Abebooks £11-85

Dad, Best Wishes +

C000244533

JULES VERNE

Backwards
to
Britain

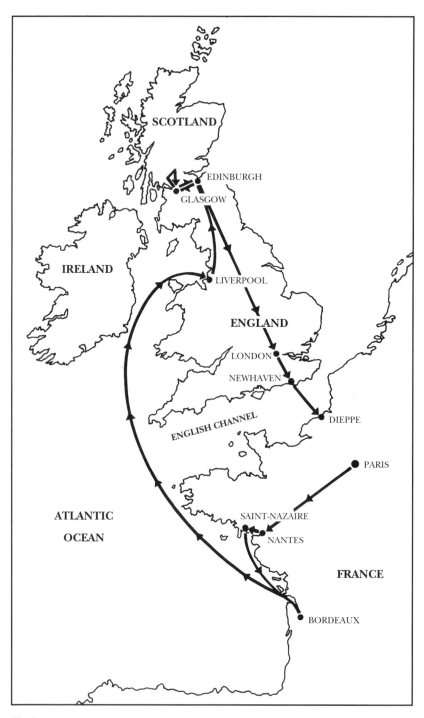

The Journey

JULES VERNE

Backwards to Britain

Chambers

EDINBURGH   NEW YORK

Published 1992 by W & R Chambers Limited
43–45 Annandale Street, Edinburgh EH7 4AZ

First published in France as
Voyage à reculons en Angleterre et en Ecosse by
le cherche midi 1989
Manuscrit in édit appartenant à la Ville de Nantes
Editor of French edition: Christian Robin
Consultant editor of English edition: William Butcher

Translated into English by Janice Valls-Russell

British Library Cataloguing in Publication Data
A catalogue record for this book is available from the British
Library

ISBN 0–550–17254–8

Editorial Manager Min Lee
Illustrations Musée du château des Ducs de Bretagne,
Médiathèque de Nantes
Map p. ii John Marshall
Cover design by Art Dept
Typeset by Buccleuch Printers Limited, Hawick
Printed in England by Clays Ltd, St Ives, plc

Contents

Introduction

Backwards to Britain is a time-bomb. It proves that Verne is not a science-fiction author; it reveals the poetic and literary sensibilities of his writing; and it shows that Scotland was always his first love.

The author of *Journey to the Centre of the Earth, Twenty Thousand Leagues under the Sea* and *Around the World in Eighty Days* still has an image problem in Britain. The works of the best-selling novelist of all time are now recognized on the Continent as authentic, mainstream literature. Thirty or so books have been written studying the *Extraordinary Journeys*, plus a good score of doctorates. Twenty-two miles away, the world's most translated writer remains an invisible man.

It seems a little curious, then, that Verne's style and vision should have been formed in part by his experiences in Britain. More curious still, on reading the first book he wrote. Composed in his early thirties, this is no preparation for greater things, but springs forth fully-formed, an artistic achievement in its own right.

Verne was proud of his Scots ancestry. His mother's maiden name, Allotte de la Fuÿe, came from an archer, Allott, who joined Louis XI's Scottish Guard, earning the aristocratic prerogative of keeping a 'fuie' ('dovecote'), plus a 'de' in his name. Verne's first novel was set in Empire territory, the second one appeared as *The British on the North Pole* (1864), and a score of others had British heroes. The Scottish settings of *The Child of the Cavern* (1877) and *The Green Ray* (1882) were about as close to home as his exoticism-seeking ever got.

Voyage en Angleterre et en Ecosse ('Backwards to Britain') is a lightly fictionalized account of Verne's first trip outside France, in 1859. It was rejected, however, by his publisher Hetzel in favour of the more topical *Five Weeks in a Balloon* (1863). It appeared only in 1989, the last of Verne's complete prose works to be published.

The volume starts by viewing Scotland in late-Romantic mode, as the centre of the dreams of 'Jacques' and 'Jonathan' (Verne and his friend Hignard). After waiting impatiently in France for over a fortnight, the two travel to Liverpool. They disembark to shocking, Dickensian conditions, including child prostitution. Following a virtuoso description of the docks, they travel on to Edinburgh.

They awake to Arthur's Seat and medieval ten-storey houses. Jacques claims never to have seen a 'mountain' or a 'loch' before and is completely bowled over by 'the terrible poetry of old Scotland'. From this point on, a litany of architecture, literature, food and ale flows from his amazed pen. The counter-weighted windows, the pretentious banks, the fetid slums, the broad avenue up the Queen's Park; verdant cemeteries and exotic botanical gardens, a royal 'pleasure-château' and the New Town with its arched 'bridges' to the front doors. A whole new world.

Verne falls for a local lass, Amelia; on her advice they sail up the Forth towards Stirling, Glasgow and Loch Katrine. They discover a landscape that *is* history, with its 'savage, melancholy and plaintive' nature, its 'sublime beauties', its people full of 'abnegation and devotion'.

Many of the major Vernian themes are already visible: the haunting music, the technology-literature link – Scott's and Watt's statues are interchangeable – the 'sinuosities' of Loch Lomond, hiding-place for untold mysteries; and above all the dream of the North, the root of Captain Hatteras's Polar suicide and of the lines-on-a-map generation of half-a-dozen novels. The savage grandeur of the Falls of Oversnaid prefigures that of Fingal's Cave in *The Green Ray*, the Greenwich Footway Tunnel strangely resembles the route from Iceland down towards the centre of the Earth, and the fine canvases and comfortable toilets in a windswept Fife wilderness brilliantly anticipate Nemo's *salon* with its perfect plumbing amidst the ranging depths.

Verne's northern urge is abruptly curtailed after only a day in the Highlands. Each successive stage of the departure, Mary, Queen of Scots-style, breaks his heart. After Linlithgow Castle, the Pentlands and the Water of Leith, an overnight journey to London and consolation in the imperial monuments and a performance of *Macbeth*. Paris, concludes Verne, is where 'the real journey begins, for imagination will now be our guide, and we will travel only in our memories'.

Backwards to Britain is a young man's work, full of humorous exaggeration and enthusiasm – even if melancholy, decay, murder and suicide also abound. It reveals the fascination with travel that is Verne's fundamental driving force. It also forms a hymn to Walter Scott, with each successive town, loch and hillside coloured by *The Heart of Midlothian* or *Rob Roy*.

Verne clearly anticipated the threat of tourism, in his hell-is-other-people descent to London, but also in casual remarks like the trippers' 'exogenous crinolines': over-sized and foreign to the sober Highland spirit. Trains are appreciated when they fit into the landscape, contributing to the gothic Romanticism of the Border country. But they autocratically cut across the London skyline, and they move too quickly for the Queen to be more than a blur or for the Crystal Palace even to be named.

Ben Lomond constitutes the true hero of the book, mentioned on page one and repeatedly thereafter. And the Forth is its handmaiden, River and Firth, faithfully guiding the two friends through the countryside. Every water-course in the following books will imitate its combination of purposeful direction and open-sea freedom; and every subsequent mountain will have to have its own pet stream, even if only of boiling lava.

But it is not as if Verne stays within the conventional limits of mid-nineteenth-century travel writing. He slips in literary devices that seem more typical of later writing. Thus many anagrams of the word 'verne' appear in the French text, and, more generally, there are many written documents *within* Verne's own text. Both devices surreptitiously refer back to the status of the text as text and therefore point to the author, constituting a discrete 'self-reference' that will be visible in many experimental writers of the twentieth century.

Backwards to Britain is similarly governed by many persistent metaphors, especially those establishing equivalences between machines and living beings. Thus trains whinny and bolt, and try to throw themselves off the rails. A ship beats its wings, groans, and roars, is 'out of breath, . . . has a weak chest'. Masts or industrial chimneys appear as bristling forests. One machine plays music on its own; and another will possibly serve as a device to automatically convert the natives of the South Seas.

The artificial and the natural, the biological and the mineral continuously switch places. Streets are tributaries for Verne, and their architecture is in perpetual 'efflorescence': mere stones are permanently springing to life. Buildings finish up 'spreading themselves out, squaring their shoulders, or casually reclining'. As if to compensate, the land displays inviting cavities and rumps, and it is a 'poetry of stones'. In Verne's imagination, mountains, although fleshless, have heads, feet and flanks, are kings. They kill trees, and these trees hang human beings. Humanity, in consequence, seems to be on the bottom rung of evolution: its members are described as mere 'inert machines'.

The ultimate mechanical metaphor, sex, throbs everywhere in the text. Jacques frantically stabs with his compasses at the map of Scotland; and exploited seamstresses appear without petticoats and blouses. But the nameless activity is most interesting when *re*-metaphorized. In Verne, ships 'couple in the middle of the river', and the already living steam-*cranes* are also steam-driven sluts ('*grues à vapeur*'). A tart has creamy plums hidden in its moist, golden sides, 'loves are rinsed in gin and brandy', girls seem ripe for plucking, 'bride' and 'bread' are interchangeable, sandwich-men parade, freshly-guillotined heads lie like bloody roast-beef. Food seems to form an eminently satisfying substitute for sex, with a strong cannibalistic streak never far from the Vernian imagination. Underneath the apparently simple text, then, there are all sorts of illicit goings-on.

In conclusion, Verne is much more complex than his reputation in Britain will allow. In particular, his literary devices serve to avoid some of the oppositions characteristic of his age. The Romantic vision of transcendental ideas and the Realist transcription of mere things, purplest passion and materialistic modernity are partly reconciled into Verne's distinctive 'world-view'. So is the gulf between humanity and its environment, with man's dominance of nature abolished and the whole physical world brought exuberantly and animistically to life.

Verne's devices also help to solve the problem of the writer. These hidden mechanisms enable him to comment indirectly on what he sees, without revealing his own vulnerability. The aim of both travel and adventure writings is in this way achieved: being both personal and impersonal, a semi-detached involvement, masking oneself behind one's own exposed viscera. *Backwards to Britain*, in sum, constitutes the author's artistic manifesto, a concise statement of intent for the whole of the next sixty years.

Verne's reputation somehow got misplaced at the beginning, due to literary snobbery and to the truncated, howler-full 'translations'. As a result, this lost manuscript, this un-Hetzel-censored book, this truly Extraordinary Journey, has never before been published in English. The Count of the North has been in a third-class cattle-truck for well over a century now, obliviously riding to the Highlands under a pouring umbrella. But the time-capsule laid down in 1859 can now finally be opened.

Backwards to Britain will surely transform the conventional wisdom on Jules Verne.

William Butcher
Vocational Training Council,
Hong Kong
May 1992

A paragraph of Jules Verne's autograph manuscript (chapter 14)

Note on the text

The French text of 1989 corrects some of the spelling and other mistakes in the manuscript. It also contains useful annotations of the changes Verne himself made to the manuscript, virtually all of which can be considered improvements. A few of the most interesting amendments have been indicated in the endnotes of the present edition (marked 'MS', the text between inverted commas (' ') being the manuscript text *before* Verne's amendments).

The title of the manuscript, on a separate page, was *Voyage en Angleterre et en Ecosse*, and this was clearly the author's intention, for it is repeated at the head of the text (as *Essai de voyage en Angleterre et en Ecosse*). The words 'à reculons', which had originally formed part of the title, are crossed out. The French edition was published under the title *Voyage à reculons en Angleterre et en Ecosse*, which has been translated as *Backwards to Britain*.

In the French text Verne uses a large number of English words, names and phrases, which are often indicated here by the use of italics or inverted commas. Many of the remaining errors have been corrected in the present text, such as 'Prince's Street', 'Grass Market', 'la rue Saint-Georges' (for 'George Street'), 'le jardin de la reine' ('Queen Street Gardens'), 'Charleston' ('Charlestown'), and so on. Verne wrote some of the names as 'S . . .' or 'O . . .', so as to protect the anonymity of the people concerned, but it has seemed appropriate here to put the full names, 'Smily' (*sic*) and 'Oakley' ('*Ockley*', in the French edition, is a mistake), and similarly '185.' has been replaced by '1859'.

The chapter headings used here are not Jules Verne's, but have been added by the publisher.

1

How it all began

'I F THERE IS ANYONE in France who has not made, or cannot make, a journey to Scotland, I would recommend instead a visit to the Upper Franche-Comté, where he will find ample compensation. The sky may be less misty, the arbitrary movements and shapes of clouds less picturesque and outlandish than in Fingal's melancholy kingdom; these minor differences excepted, there is much similarity between the two regions.' Such was Charles Nodier's advice to future generations in his *Fantaisies du dériseur sensé* (Fantasies of the Hard-headed Sceptic).[1]

Jacques Lavaret mused for some time over the pleasant storyteller's words. They had amazed him at first, since his keenest wish was to visit the homeland of Walter Scott, bend his ear to the bluff sounds of the Gaelic tongue, sniff the salutary fogs of old Caledonia — in short, soak in with all his senses the poetic essence of that enchanted land. Yet here was an intelligent man, a conscientious writer, a respected member of the French Academy, telling him in the right and proper style: 'Don't bother! Lons-le-Saunier is a fine substitute for the wonders of Edinburgh; the Jura Mountains are more than a match for Scotland's cloud-capped Ben Lomond'.

Amazement, however, soon yielded to reflection and Jacques decided that Charles Nodier's advice had been meant as a joke. For it is much easier to travel to Scotland than to Franche-Comté; and whereas one must have a pressing reason, a powerful motive to go to Vesoul, all one needs to wander north of the Clyde and the Tweed are good humour, an appetite for change, a bright idea on getting up one morning and a touch of fantasy.

Jacques smiled to himself as he closed the book. Since his many occupations left him no time to visit the Franche-Comté, he decided to visit Scotland instead. Here then is how this voyage came to be — how it almost never happened.

One day in July 1859, Jacques's closest friend Jonathan Savournon, a respected composer, said to him unexpectedly:

'Jacques, an English company has offered me a cabin in one of its steamers, which trades between Saint-Nazaire and Liverpool. I can take a friend with me. Would you like to come along?'

'I can take a friend with me. Would you like to come along?' (p. 2)

Jacques was so excited his reply choked on his lips.

'From Liverpool, we'd go on to Scotland,' Jonathan went on.

'Scotland!' Jacques had found his voice again. 'Scotland! When do we leave? Have I time to finish my cigar?'

'Steady!' Jonathan's more restrained temperament contrasted with his friend's impulsiveness. 'The engines aren't stoked yet.'

'Yes, but when do we leave?'

'In a month. Sometime between 30 July and 2 August.'

Jacques hugged Jonathan boisterously. The composer withstood the shock with the fortitude of a man used to braving the full force of an orchestral onslaught.

'Tell me, to what do we owe this good fortune?'

'It's quite simple.'

'Everything sublime is simple.'

'My brother,' Jonathan said, 'does business with this company. He regularly uses their ships to send merchandise to England. The ships used to take on passengers and are fitted out accordingly, but now they only carry freight. We'll be the only passengers on board.'

'The only passengers!' Jacques said. 'Why, that's like being royalty! Let's travel incognito, under assumed names, the way kings do. I'll be the *Comte du Nord*, like Paul I; you can be Mr Corby, like Louis-Philippe.'[2]

'As you wish,' the musician replied.

'Do you know the names of the steamers?' Jacques already saw himself on board.

'Yes, there are three: the *Beaver*, the *Hamburg* and the *Saint-Elmot*.'

'What names! What splendid names! Tell me, are they propeller-driven steamers? If so, I will never ask for anything else.'

'I've no idea. What does it matter anyway?'

'What does it matter! Do you mean you don't understand?'

'Frankly, no.'

'No! Well then, my friend, I won't tell you! Things like that can't be explained.'

And that is how their famous journey to Scotland came about. Jacques Lavaret's enthusiasm was easy to understand: until then, he had never left Paris, that unpleasant hole. Henceforth, his whole existence was encapsulated in one sweet word: Scotland. He did not lose a moment; since he knew no English, he did his utmost not to learn it, not wanting, as Balzac put it, to encumber himself with two words for one idea. Instead he reread his Walter Scott in French. He entered the homes of the Lowland gentry on the Antiquary's arm; Rob Roy's horse swept him into the heart of the rebellious clans; and the Duke of Argyle's voice could not extricate him from the Edinburgh Tolbooth. That long month of July was well spent, even though the hours seemed to him to drag on into days, the minutes into hours. Fortunately, his friend Charles Dickens entrusted him to good old Nicholas Nickleby and to kindly Mr Pickwick, who is a close relative of the philosophical Shandy.[3] Together, they initiated him into the arcane manners and customs of the various castes that constitute British society. As for Messrs Louis Enault and Francis Wey, they had naturally published their works on Britain solely to please Jacques.[4] As we can see, he received sound guidance. All these entrancing texts set Jacques's imagination ablaze and he wondered whether he shouldn't join the Royal Geographical Society.[5] It goes without saying that the map of Scotland in his Malte-Brun Atlas[6] needs replacing: it has been perforated through and through by the frenzied stabbing of his compasses.

Notes

[1] This quotation is not strictly speaking from any of the four tales that make up the *Cycle du dériseur sensé* (in *Contes*, Paris, Garnier, 1963, édition P-G Castex, pp 399–462). It is taken, with slight alterations, from the short story 'Marionnettes', Part 2, chapter 3, pp 420–1 of the Charpentier edition of Nodier's *Nouvelles*, Paris 1850, where it is typographically included in the *Cycle*.

[2] *Comte du Nord*: this was the name assumed by the future Tsar of Russia, Paul I (1754–1801), when in 1780 he planned to visit Poland, Germany, Italy, France and Holland in the company of his wife, Sophia Dorothea of Württemberg.

Mr Corby: this was the pseudonym chosen by the future king of France, Louis-Philippe [who reigned from 1830 to 1848], when he was forced to leave the Swiss Canton of Grisons, where he was teaching mathematics under an assumed name. He joined Montesquiou's army on foot, carrying a knapsack, then travelled on to Sweden.

[3] Dickens was one of Verne's literary passions, and is referred to in all the interviews Verne gave. Shandy refers of course to Sterne's novel *Tristram Shandy*.

[4] *Enault* (Hénaut in Verne's manuscript). Louis Enault (1824–1900) was born in the *département* of Calvados and studied law in Paris. On the basis of his exile from France (1848–51), he wrote *Angleterre, Ecosse, Irlande, voyage pittoresque* (England, Scotland, Ireland: a Picturesque Journey), published by Morizot in Paris in 1859.

Francis Wey was born in 1812 in Besançon (d. 1882). An enthusiastic walker, he travelled across Belgium, Holland, Switzerland, the British Isles, the Rhineland, Provence and Savoie, bringing home accounts which he published. Verne draws on *Les Anglais chez eux: esquisses de moeurs et de voyage*, ('A Frenchman sees the English in the Fifties') which was serialized between November 1850 and May 1851 in the Musée des familles, before being published in one volume in 1854.

[5] The opening scene of *Cinq semaines en ballon* ('Five Weeks in a Balloon') takes place at the Royal Geographical Society.

[6] *Atlas de Malte-Brun: Atlas complet du précis de la Géographie universelle* (Malte-Brun's Atlas: a Complete Atlas of the Précis of Universal Geography), published in 1837 by André et Lenomant (Paris). Verne's enthusiasm for maps and engravings is already apparent here. Geography was indeed the only scientific field where his knowledge was never challenged in his lifetime. Victor Adolphe Malte-Brun provided the map for C Thierry-Mieg's *Six Semaines en Afrique* (1861–2) (Six Weeks in Africa), probably the source of the title of Verne's African *Five Weeks in a Balloon*.

2

A boat that never comes

ONE OF THE STEAMERS was scheduled to dock in Saint-Nazaire on 25 July. Jacques did some careful arithmetic. By mentally allowing the valiant ship seven days to unload and reload, he decided that it should be weighing anchor by 1 August at the latest. Jonathan Savournon knew enough English for his personal use and, repressing the songs of joy that bubbled in his chest, he kept up a regular correspondence with Mr Daunt, the director of the Liverpool company. He soon informed Jacques that the ship put at their disposal was the *Hamburg*, from Dundee. It had just left Liverpool under the command of Captain Speedy and was heading for France.

The exciting moment was approaching. Jacques could not sleep. At last, the long-awaited date, 25 July, arrived in Paris and Saint-Nazaire,

He began paying assiduous visits to a confectioner in the rue Vivienne and a baker in the Passage des Panoramas. (p. 6)

but the Hamburg, alas, did not. Jacques could not bear it. He considered that the English company had defaulted on all its promises and threatened to declare it bankrupt! He persuaded his friend Jonathan to set off immediately for Nantes and Saint-Nazaire in order to watch the French coast.

Jonathan left Paris on 27 July and, awaiting his summons, Jacques hurriedly saw to his final preparations.

The first task was to obtain a passport to travel abroad, so Jacques looked for two people who could answer for him before the police *commissaire*. That was when he began paying assiduous visits to a confectioner of the rue Vivienne and a baker in the Passage des Panoramas. A terrible struggle was raging at the time between their eminent corporations on the issue of *éclairs* and *savarins*, which the bakers were making to the confectioners' disadvantage; as a result, the moment the two rivals met, they began to hurl at each other all the invective specific to the flour trade. Jacques, however, restrained them by threatening to tell the '*policemen*' — as in his anglomania he insisted on calling the *agents de police*.¹ With no further incident he brought his two witnesses before the *commissaire* – or, as Jacques would say, the '*sheriff*' – where the two tradesmen were able to testify to his morality, since he had never stolen anything from their shops. Jacques received the necessary authorization to contribute ten francs to the government coffers and thus obtain the right to travel outside France. He then went

The cab drove him to Orléans railway station. (p. 8)

The engine whistled, whinnied and bolted. (p. 8)

to the *préfecture* of the Seine — for Jacques '*the lord mayor's parlour*' — where he boldly requested a passport for the British Isles. His description was taken down by an old, myopic clerk whom the progress of civilization would one day replace by an officially designated photographer. Jacques entrusted his passport to an obliging official who, for two francs, undertook to obtain the necessary visas and authorizations from the respective embassies. He was even so kind as to bring back personally this important document which was now fully in order.

Jacques piously kissed his passport; nothing now stood in his way. On the Saturday morning, 30 July, he received a letter from good old Jonathan informing him that the *Hamburg* had not yet been sighted but was due at any moment.

Jacques hesitated no longer. He was anxious to leave Paris, its heavy climate, its ammoniacal atmosphere, its budding public gardens and the tropical forest of buildings that had just been planted around the Stock Exchange, the territory of the faithful, endlessly scurrying, Giaffirs of the powerful Harun-al-Rothschild.[2]

Jacques fastened his case which was crammed with utterly useless and cumbersome objects. He slipped his umbrella into its oilcloth tunic; over his shoulder he slung his travelling rug, which portrayed a yellow tiger on a red background; he donned the inevitable cap of the dedicated tourist; and jumped into a hackney carriage.

7

By the simplest laws of locomotion, the cab drove him to Orléans railway station. After buying a seat, he registered his luggage and, shrewd man that he was, planted himself in the first coach so as to arrive all the sooner. The bell rang; the engine whistled, whinnied and bolted, while a barrel-organ on Austerlitz Bridge sighed to the 'Miserere' of *Il Trovatore*.[3]

Notes

[1] This may be seen as a light-hearted draft of the *casus belli* which opposes three groups in *Voyages extraordinaires*, (the 'Extraordinary Journeys'), Virgamenians and Quinquendonians in *Une fantaisie du Docteur Ox* ('Dr Ox's Experiment'), port watch and starboard watch in *L'Île à hélice* ('Propeller Island') and partisans of lighter-or-heavier-than-air in *Robur-le-conquérant* ('Clipper of the Clouds').

[2] This is a reference to the Caliph Harun-al-Rashid and his Vizier Giaffir, in the *Arabian Nights* (thirty-third night).

[3] Verdi's *Il Trovatore* was performed in the Paris Opera in January 1857, in a version that differs somewhat from the present-day one. The *Miserere* is sung in Act IV, scene 1. Later, Verne became quite a fan of Verdi's.

3

In which the two friends see Nantes

JACQUES HAD LEFT PARIS at eight in the evening. The next morning, as soon as he reached Nantes, he took a cab to where Jonathan was staying. Jonathan was so soundly asleep that Jacques had an almighty struggle to wake him.

'How can you sleep?' Jacques cried. 'Hasn't the *Hamburg* arrived?'

'You'll have to be very brave, old thing,' Jonathan replied.

Jacques shuddered. 'What's happened?'

'The *Hamburg* won't be coming to Saint-Nazaire.'

The next morning, he reached Nantes. (p. 9)

'What?!'

'Here's a letter from Mr Daunt,' Jonathan said as he handed Jacques a dismal-looking document.

'But are you sure you understand this terrible English?'

'Listen. From Liverpool the *Hamburg* had to go to Glasgow to complete its load, which means a few days' delay.'

'But then it will sail south again?'

'Of course. It's expected to dock on the 4 or 5 August — '

'In Saint-Nazaire?'

'No. Bordeaux.'

Jacques relaxed.

'So let's go to Bordeaux. There's a steamboat service twice a week between Nantes and Bordeaux. We haven't a minute to lose.'

'We've got plenty of time,' Jonathan said.

'What if we miss the *Hamburg*? You know it wouldn't wait for us. Come on, don't argue with me. Let's go! What could be more beautiful than the sea?'

Jonathan winced. The beauty of the sea intimidated him rather, but as he had no hope of being able to travel by land to Scotland, he resigned himself to this introductory passage from Nantes to Bordeaux.

The ship was not due to sail before Tuesday, with the evening tide. The two friends went to book their passages at an office in the harbour, known locally as 'the Ditch'. They learned that two steamers, the *Comte d'Erlon*, a paddle-boat, and the *Comtesse de Frecheville*, a single-screw ship, would be getting up steam for Bordeaux three days later.

The two friends went to book their passages at an office in the harbour, known locally as 'The Ditch'. (p. 10)

Jacques naturally opted for the *Comtesse* but promptly abandoned her on learning that her companion, the *Comte*, would be weighing anchor an hour earlier. He refused to change his mind even after being warned that the *Comtesse* travelled faster than the *Comte*.

'I'm not worried about arriving quickly,' he said. 'My main concern is to get going.'

And Jonathan, who had a weak spot for the *Comtesse*, had to give in.

Sunday, Monday and Tuesday dragged out in deadly boredom. The two visitors tried to kill time by visiting the city, but time has a tough hide in Nantes and is not that easy to kill. Nevertheless, the bustle in the harbour, the arrival with every tide of brigs, schooners, coasting vessels and sardine boats gave Jacques thrills of ecstasy and Jonathan bouts of nausea. Jacques was fascinated by the shipyards, whence magnificent

The chapel where the wedding of Louis XIII and Anne of Austria was celebrated. (p. 11)

clippers are launched in great numbers, and it required all his friend's persuasiveness to drag him away in search of interesting architecture, be it ancient or modern. Jonathan enjoyed their visit to the château of the Dukes of Brittany, which has a chapel where the wedding of Louis XIII and Anne of Austria was celebrated. He shuddered when he realized how the historic ruins had been restored by the city council: the chapel's upper gallery had been entirely rebuilt in gleaming white stone.

'The restorers bungled it rather, don't you think?' Jonathan said.

'That's putting it mildly,' Jacques said. 'Shall we move on?'

They reached the cathedral, which has been spared by the architects of Nantes, mainly because the government has been working on its completion during the past ten years at an economic snail's pace. Overall, the building does not appear outstanding. The nave, however, is elegant and impressively high. The roof is supported on prismatic pillars of a bold, attractive design, with finely chiselled ribs that fan out to form

The nave is elegant and impressively high. (p. 12)

the keystones. The windows on the south side date from the flamboyant fourteenth-century Gothic which preceded the Renaissance; while the main porch is well worth seeing. It is a magnificent page written in splendid medieval hieroglyphics that equal the storks and ibises of ancient Egypt.

Neither Jacques nor Jonathan regretted the rewarding hours they spent there.

From medieval remains they moved on to contemporary architecture. That proved more difficult. Neither the theatre nor the stock exchange could pretend to modernity. But Jonathan was eager to see what present-day taste could produce in a provincial capital like Nantes, and in due course he was not disappointed.

The lawcourts. (p. 13)

At the end of a long street he caught sight of a building with an impressive façade.

'What's that?' he asked.

'Why, a monument, of course!' replied Jacques.

'What kind of monument?'

'A theatre! Although I wouldn't be surprised to find it's a stock exchange, unless, of course, it's a railway station!'

'It can't be.'

'No, of course. Aren't we stupid? Those are the lawcourts.'

'How can you tell?'

'Why, it says so – in gold lettering!'

And indeed, subtle man that he was, the architect had given his building a name, just like the painter Orbanga who, having painted a cock, wrote 'This is a cock'. Like so many contemporary buildings the lawcourts of Nantes were of little interest and Jonathan would not have given the façade a second glance but for the peculiar design of the stone steps. The flight of steps leading up to the main hall was obviously designed not for the public but for the half dozen columns that climb up it – to the Assizes, one imagines, which is what the wretched things deserve. Instead, however, they are left standing at the top, since they are prevented from entering the building by the bridging arch they carry on their heads, which shelters a statue of Justice in an advanced state of pregnancy.

Those were the attractions Nantes had to offer the two Parisians, who spent three days sightseeing with good grace, until Tuesday evening arrived.

4

First time on board

A LIVELY CROWD lined the quayside of the Ditch. The two steamers, the *Comte* and the *Comtesse*, were wreathed in smoke and shivered from stem to stern. The Stock Exchange clock chimed six.

Jacques and Jonathan were already on board and had chosen their berths for the night. Jacques could not keep still; he came and went, laughing with nervous excitement, sat down and sprang up again a hundred times, leaned over the rails to watch the flowing water with a thrill in his heart, before dashing off to admire the engine room and the loud throb of its boiler. He marvelled at the powerful cylinders and the pistons that would soon be in motion; then he returned to the stern, where he stood at the wheel, placing his hand on it as if he were in command. He was anxious to exchange a few words with the captain of

Neither the theatre nor the stock exchange could pretend to modernity. (p. 12)

the *Comte d'Erlon*, but the man was too busy supervising the loading of his cargo, a task which took until eight in the evening.

Jonathan was more relaxed and his musings took a different course; the idea of spending twenty-four hours on board this ship seemed anything but thrilling.

'In any case I think it's crazy to start our journey to Scotland by travelling south to Bordeaux.'

'Not at all,' Jacques retorted. 'All roads lead to Rome – as they say in Piedmont.'

At last all the passengers were on board. The captain gave orders and the paddle-wheels jerked into action. After riding the wind for a while, the ship found the current and steered swiftly through the throng of ships in the harbour.

Jacques emitted a deep sigh of contentment.

A dozen leagues[1] separate Nantes from St-Nazaire, which is on the estuary of the Loire. When the current is right the distance is easily covered in a few hours. Downstream from Nantes, however, the riverbed is obstructed with sand-bars and the ebb tide leaves only a narrow twisting channel between them. Had the *Comte* moved off at the turn of the tide, it would have been in no danger of running aground. But its departure had been delayed and the captain was not sure of being able to cross the Indret narrows.

'Once we're through, nothing can delay us,' he said.

Jacques gazed at the old sea-dog with respect and admiration. 'Which means we can be in Bordeaux –'

'By tomorrow evening.'

The paddle-wheels jerked into action. After riding the wind for a while, the ship found the current and steered swiftly through the throng of ships in the harbour. (p. 16)

16

Admittedly, it was not a fast ship, but it sped on the current. Outside Nantes harbour, eight or nine tributaries flow into the Loire. The river broadens out in a majestic expanse and its yellowish waters break against the arches of a league-long stretch of bridges. To the left lie the peaceful island and village of Trentemoult, whose peculiar-looking inhabitants are said to have preserved their primitive customs and to marry only among themselves. To the right, the steeple of Chantenay darts its sharp spire into the evening mist.[2] The two friends could barely make out the vague contours of the hills as the ship sailed past Roche-Maurice and the Haute-Indre. A distant rumbling, a black cloud, stark against the shades of the evening sky, plumes of flame waving from the tops of tall factory stacks, an atmosphere thick with the tarry emanations of coal: the ship was approaching Indret and the Basse-Indre.[3]

An atmosphere thick with the tarry emanations of coal: the ship was approaching Indret and the Basse-Indre. (p. 17)

Formerly a gun foundry,[4] Indret has become an important centre for the manufacture of government-commissioned steam engines. The hill overlooking the town from the left bank is sufficiently high to offer a view over the surrounding countryside and beyond. But Jacques gave dry land only a passing glance, for the decisive channel through the shallows lay just ahead. Standing on the bridge slung between the two paddle boxes, the captain supervised the ship's progress; it reduced speed and steam whistled through the half-open valves. Jacques was as tense as if they had been approaching the dangerous shores of Vanikoro. Suddenly there was a violent shudder as the keel scraped bottom, but the paddles hauled the ship through.

17

'We did it!' Jacques exclaimed.

'Yes,' the captain said. 'Half an hour later we'd have been stuck. But we're clear now.'

'Do you hear that, Jonathan?'

'In that case, let's tuck ourselves into bed – it'll be a tight fit – it's more like a drawer than a bed.'

'Well, it's part of the delights of life on board.'

They went down to the saloon, where some passengers had already settled down for the night. The room had red divans along the walls: in former times they had been fitted with deep recesses into which the passengers climbed, and they lay there, trying to sleep amid the groaning woodwork and creaking riggings.

An hour later a violent shudder tossed them out of their berths and Jonathan found himself sitting on the face of an old sailor stretched out on the divan below. The worthy son of Amphitrite never even stirred or awoke.

'What's happened?' Jonathan asked as he removed himself from his somewhat rugged seat.

'We're grounded,' Jacques said. His words were echoed by yells without.

The captain dashed out of his cabin, cursing. 'Well, that's it for the night,' he said. 'We're stuck until the next tide.'

Jonathan sighed. 'Ah well, we'll only be twelve hours late.'

Jacques hurried on deck. The ship was aground and lurching sideways to port – these nautical expressions went straight to his heart and fully made up for any disappointment at the delay.

Having skilfully crossed the Indret narrows, the captain had overlooked the Pellerin shallows. The water was so low that he had to

Formerly a gun foundry, Indret has become an important centre for the manufacture of government-commissioned steam engines. (p. 17)

abandon all hopes of refloating the ship before the morning tide, so on his orders the fires were banked, releasing torrents of steam. The night was dark and the riverbanks were barely visible. Jacques remained on deck for a moment, trying to pierce the shadows, before rejoining his friend, who had already clambered back into his berth over the still-sleeping sailor.

Notes

[1] One league = 3.456 statute miles.

[2] It was near the church of Saint-Martin de Chantenay that Pierre Verne bought a property around 1838. His wife and children spent many holidays there. It was there that Verne wrote or finished several of his well-known novels, such as *Les Enfants du Capitaine Grant* (Captain Grant's Children), *Vingt mille lieues sous les mers* ('Twenty Thousand Leagues Under the Sea') and *Autour de la Lune* ('Round the Moon'). In an interview given in 1893 he said 'I never went to Chantenay without entering the government machine factory of Indret, and standing for hours together watching the machines at work. This task has remained with me all my life'.

[3] Verne sailed down the Loire several times in his yachts. In *Souvenirs d'enfance et de jeunesse* ('Memoirs of Childhood and Youth') (*Cahiers de l'Herne*, Paris, 1974, pp 59–61), he describes an outing at the age of twelve in a steamship which left a lasting impression. This outing is associated with several experiences of Crusoe-like adventures on the islands of the Loire. Sailing down a river is a favourite setting in novels such as *La Jangada* ('The Giant Raft'), *Le Superbe Orénoque* ('The Superb Orinoco'), *Famille-sans-nom* ('A Family without a Name'), *Le Pilote du Danube* ('The Danube Pilot'), and *Le Secret de Wilhelm Storitz* ('The Secret of Wilhelm Storitz').

[4] *a gun foundry*: Several plots of the *Voyages extraordinaires* ('Extraordinary Journeys') stress the importance of artillery: the Cycle of the Gun-Club – *De la Terre à la Lune* ('From the Earth to the Moon'), *Autour de la Lune* ('Round the Moon'), *Sens dessus dessous* ('Topsy-Turvey') – as well as the opening of *Vingt mille lieues sous les mers* ('Twenty Thousand Leagues under the Sea'), *Les Cinq cents millions de la Bégum* ('The Begum's Fortune'), and *Face au drapeau* ('For the Flag').

5

Jonathan is seasick

THE SUN RISES early in August, but Jacques was up even earlier. At four in the morning he went on deck, pulling along the hapless, bleary-eyed Jonathan who did not see why he should already be up and about. On Jacques's request two cups of dubious-looking coffee were brought to them.

'Excellent!' he said, while his friend shuddered between each sip. 'The best coffee is undoubtedly a subtle blend of bourbon, moka and Rio Nuñez, but I don't want to denigrate this one, even though it is obviously extracted from a perennial fusiform tap root of the chicory family.'

'Trust you to wriggle out of tight corners with a definition,' Jonathan said.

Saint-Nazaire was already coming into sight at the far end of its basin at the mouth of the Loire. (p. 22)

'Definitions are useful. The truth is, I'm easy to please and I find everything perfect when I'm travelling.'

Around six o'clock the tow of the flood tide could be felt and the *Comte d'Erlon* was soon afloat and riding free. It steamed down the Loire, leaving behind Paimboeuf[1], an important administrative centre, and Donges, a small picturesque village whose old church enhances the charm of the pleasant riverside scenery. Saint-Nazaire was already coming into sight at the far end of its basin at the mouth of the Loire. Soon the passengers on board the *Comte* were greeting the new-born harbour of Saint-Nazaire, for which many citizens of Nantes fearfully

A line of water cut across the western horizon. It was the open sea. (p. 22)

predict the same prosperity as for Le Havre, which is downstream on the Seine from the older, declining Rouen. A forest of masts stood up over the embankments that enclose the docks. A line of water cut across the western horizon. It was the open sea.

When Jacques saw it, he could not help clapping his hands and calling it by its legendary names. The weather was splendid and Jonathan would have been perfectly happy, but for a continuous, sickening, ground-swell. Soon the bell called everyone down to the dining-saloon for a fairly typical steamboat lunch. The food was quite fresh and seemed to satisfy everyone. Jacques threw himself on his meal and devoured everything, including a great quantity of grilled sardines which the captain recommended to his passengers' Parisian taste-buds.[2]

'They were fished right where we are at this moment,' he said. 'You'll never taste their like again.'

'Delicious,' Jacques said. 'I would even say succulent.'

After a perfect meal, the two young men returned to the deck just as the old sailor began on his sea yarns.

The wind was in their favour so the captain ordered the sails to be unfurled. Jacques was thrilled to hear him use nautical terms, such as 'spanker' and 'foresail'. The other passengers, meanwhile, had stayed on in the saloon where, once the tables had been cleared, they began playing bezique – one of those monstrous card-games which have contributed so much to the general decline of intellectual standards. The elegant exchanges of these apparently respectable people occasionally reached the deck:

'Eighty for kings, forty for knaves, sixty for queens.'

Jacques was furious. It spoiled the Atlantic Ocean for him.

The ship was already leaving behind the dangerous reefs that mark the estuary of the Loire. The rocky heads of the Charpentier islands had sunk below the skyline and the island of Noirmoutier was fading in the sunlight. An awning had been erected over the deck to shelter passengers from the heat, but with the contempt of an experienced seaman, Jacques insisted on tanning his face, so he stretched out in a lifeboat attached to the side of the ship. Suspended over the foaming waves, his face moistened by the damp salty spray, he was too interested in everything he could see and hear to feel the slightest symptom of seasickness, an ailment he did not believe in anyway – which is an infallible way of avoiding it.

Jonathan was much less captivated by the voyage – and consequently less at ease. He had neither sea legs nor the heart of a sailor and his stomach was giving him trouble. His hands gripped the riggings with convulsive haste; his face turned white and, as his temples constricted strangely, he muttered fervent prayers to Our Lady of Nausea. Suddenly he was seen dashing to the stern and leaning overboard to deliver into the wake the secret of his sufferings.

Jacques could not help laughing, but his miserable friend did not even have the energy to be angry.

'Well,' he said, his eyes streaming and with a catch in his voice, 'I suppose it did me good. I certainly feel lighter.'

Around two o'clock the Isle of Yeu appeared on the horizon to port. The captain steered between it and the mainland and approached the island in the hope of obtaining lobster from the fishermen. One or two boats with red sails moved off from the shore, but to the cook's regret, none came near the ship. The grounding of the previous evening had upset his calculations and he was afraid of running out of food before they docked in Bordeaux.

'We'll anchor in the Garonne tomorrow morning,' the captain said confidently.

Jacques was seriously impressed by the mariner's ability to predict the end of a long journey with such precision. As they steamed past the south-eastern tip of the island, a plaintive tune reached him on the wind and he hurried over to his friend who was lost in glum contemplation.

'Listen!' Jacques said. 'Can you hear that heavenly tune on the breeze? It must be one of those primitive songs that well up from the bosom of the ocean.'

Jonathan could not resist this poetic invitation; he stood in the teeth of the wind, ready to jot down in his diary the evanescent notes of this Atlantic melody. He listened carefully. Some rustic hurdy-gurdy was playing 'Il baben del suo sorrizo', from *Il Trovatore*.[3]

'How strange – and depressing,' Jacques said. 'Don't you think?'

'I think I'm feeling twice as seasick,' Jonathan said, and he returned to his observation post at the stern.

The dinner bell sounded while they were abreast of Les Sables d'Olonne. Jonathan and a few other passengers were missing. Ships' cooks always take such desertions into account, which is fair enough. During the evening, the wind freshened and turned to the south. The sails were furled and the ship rolled and pitched inconsiderately, more vulnerable to the swell. Unable to stay in his berth, where he felt worse than ever, Jonathan wrapped himself in his travelling rug and resigned himself to a night on deck. As for Jacques, he paced up and down, a cigar in his mouth, legs apart, like a veteran seaman, to keep his balance while the night wrapped the floating machine in a cloak of shadows.

Notes

[1] Paimboeuf was where the 12-year-old Verne was said to have finished up, after his attempt to run away to sea to fetch coral for his cousin Caroline. This story, reported by his niece Marguerite Allotte de la Fuÿe, is now regarded by many as apocryphal.

[2] When on holiday in Chantenay, Verne used to send P J Hetzel, his publisher, sardines caught by the fishermen of Les Sables d'Olonne, La Turballe and Le Croisic (letter of summer 1866 [?], Bibliothèque Nationale, NAF 17004, folio 7 overleaf).

[3] From Act II, scene 2.

6

To Scotland, but backwards

SOON ALL WAS STILL on board. There were only four people left on deck: the watch, the helmsman, the old sailor and our friend Jacques.

The last two got talking and the Parisian found the old sea-dog full of useful, if not exactly fascinating knowledge. He pointed out the lighthouses on the islands of Ré and Oléron, which lit up the coast two or three leagues under the lee. Jacques could not take his eyes off those lights, now still, now revolving, which projected beams through lenses of flint-glass far over the sea.[1]

Around midnight, the young man felt overcome by drowsiness and withdrew to his berth. He was back on deck at dawn, however, in Jonathan's company, to greet the Tour de Cordouan which marks the mouth of the Gironde. The estuary is as wide there, as a sea-channel. Its calmer waters helped to revive the passengers.

'Considering this river flows through Bordeaux, I find it very placid indeed,' Jacques said.

At eight in the morning, the *Comte d'Erlon* was greeted by a pilots' launch. One pilot climbed aboard while the others sailed off in search of more incoming ships.

He was a lively little man, a good-humoured Gascon who moved, spoke and gesticulated with southern enthusiasm. His manner, appearance and Bordeaux accent appealed to Jonathan, who was beginning to relax. Whether standing on the deck or leaning on the rail, the pilot adopted graceful, instinctively artistic poses. His speech was rapid, at times onomatopoeic, and his pleasant laughter revealed a set of dazzling white teeth.

As soon as he was on board, he took over the helm from the captain who thus relinquished his responsibility. Their exchanges sounded grim and full of dark forebodings.

'The tide's very low,' the pilot said.

25

'Bah,' the captain said. 'We've got plenty of time.'

'I'm not so sure.'

'We'll stoke the engines.'

'But we're sailing into the wind.'

'Nonsense. We'll get through even so, don't worry.'

'Get through to where?' wondered Jonathan out loud.

'Come on,' said Jacques. 'The captain said we'd be in Bordeaux in a few hours. If he were the Gascon of the two, I might have my doubts. But he's a Breton, a reliable fellow. We'll be all right.'

An hour later, Jonathan was lurching about on deck; the ship had run aground on a mudbank of the Gironde, where it remained as unmovable as the earth before Galileo.

The fortress of Blaye came into sight. (p. 27)

'This is where we spend the next six hours,' the pilot said.

'I'll be damned,' the captain said.

'What was that you said about getting through, Jacques?'

'Let's go down to lunch!'

This time, all the passengers were there. The sea air had given everyone a fierce appetite. And eating helped to pass the time. The captain and the cook paled and exchanged looks of dismay. The ship had sailed from Nantes thirty-six hours earlier for a voyage scheduled to last only twenty-four. With this new delay, it seemed probable that this difficult lunch would be followed by a non-existent dinner.

'Do you think Bordeaux really exists?' Jonathan asked glumly.

'I can't swear to Bordeaux but as to its wines – certainly. Cheer up! Let's have our lunch!'

The cook was a man of imagination and he dished up mysterious scraps in a weird-looking sauce seasoned with odd condiments. Fortunately, there was no shortage of wine which coloured the tepid, cloudy water stored in the hold. In short, everyone ate eagerly without worrying about the next meal. When they had finished, some passengers resumed their never-ending bezique while the rest returned on deck.

They were stranded in an interesting stretch of the Gironde. The right bank was scarcely visible but the left shore stretched out in a huge peninsula trapped between river and ocean, where the sun's rays shine down so as to produce the excellent Médoc vintages.

At three o'clock the tug of the tide could be felt. The boiler was fired up and vigorously stoked. The paddle wheels began to turn and the ship tore itself away from the river's deep embrace. The pilot took up his observation post beside the helmsman and with his hand signalled the twists and turns of the narrow channel. The fortress of Blaye came into sight. Here, a birth that was also a political deliverance[2] occurred in 1833, saving the government of the time from an awkward crisis. Blaye is otherwise unimportant and the beach looks dry, hard and barren, without a patch of shade. One cannot help feeling that heaven's gifts were all showered on the far bank, with its Château-Margaux and Château-Laffite. Pauillac appeared next, the main port of embarkation for the Médoc wines. A kind of long jetty extends into the river to enable ships to come alongside. The banks of the Gironde drew closer together as the *Comte* steamed down towards Bordeaux. The current was swifter than it had been on the Loire, where the ship had to compete with the rising tide, and this helped the panting, wheezing engines.

'Our poor *Comte d'Erlon* has weak lungs,' Jacques said. 'I hope he doesn't run out of coal, which is like chest balm to all these steam engines.'[3]

'That would be the last straw,' Jonathan said. 'And to think this tramping down to Bordeaux is part of a journey to Scotland!'

Soon it was dinner-time and the passengers hurried down to the saloon with an eagerness that boded the cook no good. They all sat down, spread out their napkins, held out their plates to the captain at the head of the table, to receive a nauseating liquid that could be considered soup only because it was served at the beginning of the meal. After the meal it would have been dismissed as dishwater. It was in these memorable circumstances that the ship's cat vanished forever. The poor creature was strongly seasoned, but the resentful beast got its revenge in poor Jonathan's stomach. No doubt he had swallowed the claws. Rising to the occasion, the captain offered his ravenous guests a few sardines, declaring:

'Gentlemen. I didn't wan't you to reach Bordeaux without tasting these delicious *royans*,[4] which were caught in the Gironde.'

'What do you mean, *royans*!' everyone exclaimed indignantly. 'Why, they are just ordinary sardines!'

'Gentlemen, you are mistaken. These are genuine and, if I may say so, excellent *royans*.'

His guests preferred to eat them than argue about them. Jacques decided, logically enough, that sardines were *royans* in Bordeaux and *royans* were sardines in Nantes. Sailing up the Gironde had truly made a Gascon of their Breton captain.

Notes

[1] MS: over the sea. 'They sailed past the lighthouses of the islands of Ré and Oléron, not far from a small harbour where the *Comte d'Erlon* was forced to seek shelter a few weeks later. The unfortunate ship was driven into the harbour by a furious hurricane, and apparently tried to haul itself onto the quayside for when the time came to leave, there was not enough water and the poor *Comte* had to be dismembered and broken up.'
"*Disjecta membra poetae*,"* Jacques said on learning this tragic event.'
(*Disjecti membra poetae*, 'the poet's dispersed limbs' (Horace, *Satires*, Book I, satire iv), now a commonplace phrase used in all circumstances.)

[2] This is a reference to the birth on 1 April, 1833, of a daughter of the Duchess of Berry, whose father was Count Lucchesi-Palli. Verne did not like this heiress of the Bourbons, whom he attacks in one of his poems.

[3] *chest balm: pâte-regnault*, a balsamic pectoral liniment for which F L Dorvault gives the formula in his *Officine*.

[4] Sardines, named in the Bordeaux area after the small harbour of Royan, where they are caught.

7

Stopover in Bordeaux

A LONG PLUME of smoke appeared on the horizon. It came from a steamer that was rapidly approaching the *Comte d'Erlon*. It advanced with incomparable grace and speed under the smooth quiet thrust of its propeller, with its sails neatly folded on the yardarm.

'That's a handsome ship,' Jacques said. 'And she's much swifter than ours. I'd like to know her name for my log-book.'

He trained his field glasses on the ship and soon had the reply, proclaimed distinctly on the port stern, *Comtesse de Frècheville*.

'Why, it's the *Countess*!' he exclaimed.

And indeed it was. She had left Nantes twelve hours after the *Count*, and would reach Bordeaux twelve hours ahead.

'Her figure's certainly trimmer than the *Count*'s,' Jonathan said. 'What a beauty! I knew we should have entrusted ourselves to her.'

A swipe from his dinnertime cat's paw stopped his comments.

The Gironde now offered the travellers a splendid panorama. The ship had reached the Bec d'Ambès, a spit between the rivers Dordogne and Garonne which merge at this point to become the Gironde. The four converging riverbanks are covered with the lush greenery of magnificent trees. The union of the two rivers is harmonious and there is a honeymoon glow about the Bec d'Ambès. It is further downstream in life, as they approach the Atlantic, that the riverwaters quarrel like an aging couple and lash up waves of irritation.

Night was already falling. Impatient to reach the end of their journey, the passengers stood restlessly at the bow, gazing ahead at the meandering river, their disappointment growing with every swerve and bend.

'Ridiculous! Incredible! We'll never reach Bordeaux tonight. To think we've been locked up for forty-eight hours in this wretched crate.'

They complained to the captain, cross-examined the first mate, and appealed to the pilot who looked at them sarcastically.

Two more hours went by, two deathly hours which saw the ship buffeted by wind and tide. At last a few scattered lights appeared on the right bank, a few factory chimneys glowed on the left bank, and the outline of ships lying at anchor came dimly into sight in the hazy darkness. The ship was following the rocky base of a hill beside which the Paris express hurtled past, whistling. Suddenly there was a clatter of unrolling chains, the ship shuddered to an abrupt halt, steam hissed out of the boiler and the last drops of water trickled down the exhausted paddles. The ship had dropped anchor.

'Well, here we are,' Jacques said.

'Yes, but where's Bordeaux?' voices asked.

'This is Lormont,' the captain said placidly. 'One league from Bordeaux, where we will moor in the morning.'

Cursing him, all his passengers headed for their miserable berths.

As all things eventually draw to an end, even a passage from Nantes to Bordeaux, the next morning found the ship berthed before the Bordeaux customs house. After entrusting their trunks to one of the noisiest porters in sight, our two friends made for the Hôtel de Nantes, right on the harbour.

They had spent sixty hours on the *Comte d'Erlon* to find themselves 500 kilometres south of Paris.

'That's a fine start to a journey to the North,' Jonathan said.

It is easy to guess what Jacques's main concern had been as the steamer moved upstream toward Bordeaux from Lormont. He had studied the countless ships riding at anchor in the middle of the river. He was sure the *Hamburg* must be one of them. It was intolerable to think that the ship might be steaming swiftly northwards to Liverpool while the *Comte d'Erlon* wheezed painfully into Bordeaux.

As soon as their luggage had been taken to the hotel, Jacques and Jonathan returned to the harbour. They found a customs officer, whom they questioned about the arrivals and sailings of the previous days. He was an obliging man and gave them detailed information: the *Hamburg* was not listed among either the incoming or the outgoing ships of the previous days.

'My God!' Jacques looked worried. 'I hope the *Hamburg* won't decide to load up in Saint-Nazaire now we're in Bordeaux.'

'That would be dreadful,' Jonathan said. 'But let's find out what's going on. Let's call on a good Bordeaux friend of mine and pay our respects to Mr Daunt's local representative. Then we'll know what the situation is.'

These fine words needed the appropriate deeds. Having been told the way, Jacques Lavaret and Jonathan Savournon set off arm in arm for the rue Cornac.

8

Drinking in Bordeaux

IT WAS A SUNNY Friday morning. Jacques was still sleeping off a dreadful migraine which he had brought upon himself by spending the whole of the previous day watching the bright waters of the Gironde and the Garonne. When eventually he got up, Jonathan introduced him to Edmond R–, a businessman. There is no need to specify his business: lawyers, solicitors, stockbrokers, investors, magistrates, porters, journalists – everyone in Bordeaux sells wine. Everyone has a more or less well-stocked cellar and devotes himself to this pleasant trade on the side.

Edmond R– was a real son of the Garonne, with curly black hair and a strong intelligent face; of unflappable composure, he was enterprising, bold, confident, never at a loss for words and, to round off the description, lefthanded. He was overjoyed to receive the two young men and said he would be delighted to show them the city. First, though, he insisted on lunch and it was a treat to be able to sit at a well-furnished table at last and eat genuine *royans*.

Their host had alerted his wine-steward and the table was graced with slender-necked bottles filled with a seductive elixir.

It would be wrong to think that wine is drunk casually in Bordeaux. This important activity is regulated by a strict etiquette. The first wine Edmond R– served was a fifteen-year-old Clos d'Estournelle, a wine meriting careful consideration. Edmond began by pouring it into large glasses, stopping when they were a quarter full. Inviting his guests to do the same, he raised his glass to eye-level, studied the ruby liquid, observed that the wine had a generous alcoholic content and a heightened complexion, and was full-blooded, aromatic, and had a good body. He then lowered his glass, swirled its contents around slowly from right to left and faster from left to right, plunged into it the prominent wine-sniffer which Nature had generously endowed him with, and for a few minutes inhaled the delicate aromas released by his skilful rotation of the glass. After a moment of silent ecstasy, he closed his eyes to imbibe the sensuous delights which had ripened over the years in that life-enhancing beverage. That is how people drink wine in Bordeaux. There is something religious about the ceremony and evil might befall whoever would proceed differently.

Jacques found all this highly entertaining. The snag was: it slowed down the meal, and his chief interest lay in obtaining news about the *Hamburg*. So when Edmond R– offered to show them around, he insisted on being taken first of all to see Mr Daunt's agent, refusing to admire the sights of the city. He did not even spare a glance for the large Quinconces Esplanade, which happened to be crowded with the stalls of an exhibition.

When he met the shipping company's representative, he learned that Mr Daunt in person would be visiting Bordeaux shortly. As for the *Hamburg*, it had set sail from Glasgow and was expected from one day to the next. Somewhat disappointed, Jacques then allowed himself to be shown around Bordeaux.

Edmond R– had no preconceived notions about his home town. He was not at all demanding – provided his visitors showed boundless enthusiasm for the city's streets, squares, public buildings, harbour, river and surrounding region.

Ever a true musician, Jonathan's overriding interest lay in the female half of the population. So they went to a market swarming with *grisettes* – spirited working girls whose attractive madras handkerchiefs vividly set off their lively features. Most of them were dark-skinned, with gleaming

The wide streets of the new districts give Bordeaux the appearance of a large city. (p. 33)

The view from the window was splendid. (p. 34)

teeth. Their bodices were alluring, their movements graceful and vivacious, and they seemed quite ready to share their wit. But what a bustle there was in that market! What a noise! Cries, calls, bold exchanges, spicy metaphors dropping from pert, inventive lips – it was as if the water of the Garonne was rippling through those loquacious throats.

The wide streets of the new districts give Bordeaux the appearance of a large city. The theatre is impressive and overlooks an elegant square that offers easy access to the peristyle. It is a pity that the architect, Louis, did not orientate the façade towards the harbour.

Overwhelmed by a temperature of 30°C, the two visitors were exhausted and, despite Edmond's enthusiasm, Jacques could muster only a mild interest in the architectural attractions he pointed out. One thing, however, brought a smile to his face. It was the sight of local donkeys trotting gravely down the streets, strangely accoutred in cotton or linen trousers.

'All they need is a black coat, he said, 'and they would look like scholars.'

A huge number of ships was consorting, all different yet all equally splendid. (p. 34)

'It must be to protect them from the flies,' Jonathan said.

'I didn't suppose it was to go into society.'

After shaking hands with Edmond, the two Parisians went up to the room that had been prepared for them at the hotel. The view from the window was splendid. To the right, the elegant Bordeaux bridge spanned the Garonne; beyond that, the iron bridge intended to link the Orléans and Midi railway stations was already advancing over the river, encased in scaffolding. Opposite the harbour, on the far bank, the Bastide district displayed its picturesque lines of town houses and country residences. Hundreds of small boats decorated with awnings and flags plied continually between the quaysides of the two banks. To the left, the Garonne curved round the Bacalan dock, with the hills of Lormont visible on the distant horizon. And, in midriver, a huge number of ships was consorting, all different yet all equally splendid: cargo ships, American clippers, English steamers, each riding on a single anchor so that they swung on the tide and drifted gently round on the current.

9

The Bay of Arcachon

THE NEXT MORNING found Jacques and Jonathan running down to the docks to question the obliging customs officer. No news of the *Hamburg*. To occupy his guests, Edmond R– proposed an outing on the Garonne, which they accepted. They took a boat from the quay beside the Hôtel de Nantes, where a gigantic masting machine stood.

As the boat approached the Bordeaux bridge, Edmond delighted his guests with one of the tall stories of which he had an inexhaustible supply.

'I suppose you think that bridge is just a bridge,' he said.

'Why, yes.'

'Well, my friends, it's also used as military barracks.'

'Barracks!'

'And sizeable ones, too. Why, they can quarter six thousand men under that bridge.'

'Come on!' Jacques exclaimed.

'At least six thousand,' Edmond insisted.

'Don't you go doubting his figures,' Jonathan said, 'or you'll have twenty thousand men before you know where you are.'

'All right. I'll settle for six thousand Gascons.'

After admiring the bold arches of the bridge, they continued downriver towards the Bacalan wharf and on their way back followed the long quaysides as far as the Stock Exchange, a somewhat unimpressive building. Edmond took them to the cathedral, which is not listed in the annals of archaeology, and rightly so. After that, they headed for the Saint-Michel tower, which houses some highly unusual mummies, including that of a dock-hand who became a legendary figure by reputedly lifting onto his shoulders a load weighing over three thousand pounds.

'Three thousand pounds!' Jacques exclaimed, forever sceptical. 'How much do pounds and kilos weigh here in Gascony?'

After that, they headed for the Saint-Michel tower. (p. 35)

'He really lifted those three thousand pounds,' Edmond replied, 'unless it was four thousand.'

'Come on!'

'Don't provoke him, or it'll be five thousand next.'

Edmond shrugged. As a true Gascon, he saw nothing wrong with such epic facts and feats.

The day was rounded off with a visit to the theatre and a provincial performance of the *Huguenots*.[1]

Sunday 8 August passed, with still no news of their phantom ship. At a loss how to entertain his despondent guests, Edmond R– decided to take them to Arcachon. Jonathan was reluctant. He considered it ridiculous to pursue his precious journey to Scotland by plunging still further southwards, but he was outnumbered two to one, so on Monday morning they caught a local train, reaching their destination a few hours later.

The day was rounded off with a visit to the theatre. (p. 36)

The Arcachon basin is large and well worth a visit. Long, high sand dunes planted with evergreen pine-trees stretch out in pleasing lines along the shores. An invigorating smell of resin impregnates the air. Civilization is gradually taming this hitherto wild, deserted area, and Mr Coste's oyster-farms are playing their part in increasing the local population.

Between 9 and 12 August, the three tourists spent their time riding on horseback or bathing in the warm waters which become phosphorescent at night. They also had a meal at the lighthouse by the mouth of the basin, where it opens into the Bay of Biscay. That was as far south as the two young men went.

On Thursday a telegram addressed to Edmond R– by one of his employees announced the arrival of the *Hamburg*.

'We must leave at once,' Jacques said.

'But –'

'No buts! I don't want the *Hamburg* to slip away in our absence.'

'But it will need at least three or four days to unload and reload.'

'Never! Not with those Bordeaux dock-hands and steam-operated cranes. You stay if you like. I'm going.'

As always, Jonathan gave in and they left, taking Edmond who had ceased to believe the *Hamburg* really existed, with them.

On Friday the 13th,[2] the trio were back on the railway and at noon Jacques was dashing into the harbour, where he looked around for his ship. Nothing. He questioned his faithful customs officer who confirmed the arrival of the *Hamburg* but was unable to tell him where it was berthed. Jacques joined his friends for lunch on the theatre square, overjoyed that he was at last sure of sailing.

The meal was a festive occasion. Edmond treated his friends to a vintage Lur-Saluces, which he spoke of with immense respect.

'Do you know how much this wine costs?' he asked.

'No! But we'll take your word for it!'

'Well, although it isn't really done to boast about the price of things, I'll tell you: it's worth 25 000 francs a barrel.'

'I say!' Jonathan exclaimed.

'Come on!' Jacques said.

'Yessir: 25 000 francs, and that's falling short of the truth.'

'I can't believe it.'

'Look out,' Jonathan said warningly, 'he'll be telling you 40 000 francs next.'

After two hours and a most satisfying lunch, the three bosom-friends set out for the harbour finally in search of the *Hamburg*.

Notes

[1] Meyerbeer's *Huguenots* is frequently performed in Quinquendone, the small town of the eccentric Dr Ox.

[2] In 1859, 13 August was in fact a Saturday.

10

Getting under way

T HEY FOUND THE *Hamburg* berthed right in front of the Hôtel de Nantes. It was a 500-ton 90-horsepower steamer with a single screw. Rigged like a schooner, its masts tilting toward the stern, it had a trim appearance. The passengers' cabins and saloon were forward, in the deck house; this meant that they were not disturbed by the proximity of the engine-room, which was relegated abaft as is usual in English ships. An ingenious system of gangways enabled the crew to wander all over the ship without stepping on the deck, which was usually

It was a 90-horsepower steamer with a single screw. (p. 39)

covered with cargo. The wheel was on the navigation bridge amidships, so that nothing obstructed the helmsman's visibility and his gaze could encompass the whole horizon.

Jacques rapidly noted all this as, followed by his friends, he dashed on deck. Drawing on his memories of English, Jonathan asked for the captain, who appeared. He was a burly-looking Scotsman with a frank, open face. He looked like a steady sailor and a reliable comrade. A ruddy weatherbeaten complexion heightened his good-natured Caledonian features. Altogether, he was a pleasing sight. He greeted his passengers-to-be with enthusiasm and led them into the main saloon. The *waiter*, as the two Frenchmen called the steward, arrived with a huge Cheshire cheese – one foot across by two high, which he set on the table. A coffee-pot full of boiling water appeared with a big bottle of whisky and large tumblers. Despite their recent lunch, Captain Speedy's guests had to do justice to the intimidating cheese and the monumental whisky. Under the effect of that powerful drink made from grain and quite colourless, but with stimulating effects which are heightened by the addition of boiling water, Jacques felt desperately ill but his cheerfulness was undiminished. The captain had a good sense of Scottish hospitality and drink followed drink. He told Jonathan about Scotland, Edinburgh, Dundee, and the words *little girl*, *pretty girl* recurred frequently amid broad smiles of delight. Jacques, of course, did not understand a word. Even so, he found Captain Speedy to be a man of exceptional wit.

Jonathan enquired when they would be sailing, and the captain assured him that the ship would be ready to weigh anchor in three or four days' time.

Aglow with the cheese and whisky, Edmond R– had a great idea. He invited the captain to dinner that very evening. The good man promptly accepted and at the appointed hour they found themselves gathered round a splendidly laden table. How Jacques, Edmond and Jonathan were able not only to stand the sight of all the food spread out before them but also to make it disappear is a problem I leave to future generations to solve. What is sure is that the Scotsman did his dutiful best to lend them a helping fork. What a set of jaws he had! The conversation ranged widely. With an elegant, amiable air, Edmond indulged in the most appalling nonsense. The captain did not understand a word but he laughed so loudly he almost cracked the plates. The Gascon had aspired to make the Scotsman drunk. What a hope! To the vain flow of Bordeaux, Burgundy and Champagne succeeded a vain succession of cognacs and samples from the Kirsch region. Captain Speedy knocked back everything without turning a hair: the Garonne was drowned in the Clyde. At midnight the orgy ended and the young Parisians returned to their hotel, clinging to either side of the burly captain, with Jacques speaking an English he did not know and the Scotsman replying in a French he had never learned.

The next day brought a respite and no-one left his bed. On Sunday the whole area was abruptly woken up by the cannon-salvoes of 15 August, which were fired to mark the national holiday.[1] In the evening, a magnificent firework-display was due to round off the fête but in good Bordeaux style it had set itself off a few days earlier, so that, in the end, the celebrations were limited to forty-two salvoes, fired by infantrymen.

The hours trickled by, with any activity aboard the *Hamburg* proceeding so slowly that the waterline did not move. The unloaded ship rode depressingly high above water. Monday came and went, then Tuesday; it was only on Wednesday that the main cargo, which consisted of sacks of wheat, began to be loaded. The hatchways were opened and the hold started filling up. Jacques had struck up an acquaintance with a senior dock-hand who acted as interpreter and directed the arrival of the goods. He pestered the man with endless questions for the captain, all relative to the estimated date of departure. The Scotsman finally settled for Friday, whereupon Jacques would have gone aboard immediately. Jonathan, however, would not hear of it. He still had doubts – rightly so. He was growing seriously bored with the whole idea and talked of giving up that absurd, backward voyage to Scotland to travel south into the Pyrenees instead. This led to a heated discussion between the two friends, fanned by Edmond's irony and his endless jokes about the *Hamburg* and Old Caledonia. With some difficulty, Jacques persuaded Jonathan to stick to their original plan. In exchange, however, he agreed to accompany Edmond and him to the bridge of Cubzac. This took place on Thursday – a splendid day that nearly ended in disaster when they almost got stuck in the mudflats of the Dordogne. Unlike Empedocles they reached the bank in safety, losing only their sandals in the process, more fortunate, if less famous, than the philosopher of Agrigentum.

Friday arrived, but the ship was not yet loaded.[2] The captain announced that they would sail on Sunday morning without fail. The young musician thought he would go mad. Jacques clenched his teeth in irritation while Edmond indulged in senseless mimicry. During the next two days, Jacques could not keep still and on Saturday evening he insisted that they sleep on board, even though the ship was not scheduled to weigh anchor before ten in the morning. At his request, the hotel porter took their portmanteaux to the deck and Edmond promised to be there at dawn for a last handshake.

Notes

[1] During the Second Empire, 15 August was the feast-day of 'St Napoléon'.

[2] Friday – *not yet loaded* replaces 'On Friday, the vitals of the *Hamburg* were still visible above the water line. The loading had not made any progress.'

11

En route for Scotland at last

THE *HAMBURG'S* MAIN SALOON, furnished in a comfortable English style, was admirable. Ample divans lined two walls and elegant curtains graced the doors. A bookcase stood against the far wall, and a clock and a barometer indicated, side by side, the present hour and the weather to come.

On either side of the bookcase a door opened into a cabin. Each cabin contained four berths, one pair above the other, in the axis of the ship, and a sofa beneath small windows which offered a sweeping view of the sea; in the lefthand corner a washstand provided plentiful water from taps bearing the words *up, shut.*

The two passengers chose the lower berths which were fitted out with mattresses and, in the English fashion, sheets that were too short and pillows that were too narrow. With a chuckle they slipped into their bedding and Jacques fell asleep over volume three of Saint-Simon's *Mémoires.*

The engines were roaring the next morning and the *Hamburg* started manoeuvring in the harbour waters under the guidance of a thoroughly grumpy pilot who did not speak a word of English – which made his relations with Captain Speedy difficult.

The ship moved down the Garonne, but this was not yet its final departure. It stopped at the Bacalan wharf to take on more cargo. The hatches of the wheat-crammed hold were closed and covered with waterproof tarpaulins, so that the deck could receive a big load of pit props brought in two barges that rode alongside the ship.

At this point Edmond arrived to join his friends. The captain hoped to sail with the evening tide and wanted the cargo stowed as fast as possible, but it was a slow job. The wood had to be stacked so as to save space and chained down to prevent it from sliding over the deck when the ship rolled.

When he realized his friends still had some time ahead of them, Edmond proposed a meal in Lormont, which was one league

Each cabin contained four berths, one pair above the other. (p. 43)

downstream from Bacalan. He invited the captain, who preferred
however to stay on board and press on with the final preparations. The
Hamburg's boat delivered Edmond and his friends to the right bank after
they had earnestly promised to be back before the tide.

Jacques was so anxious not to miss the tide that he was positively
unpleasant throughout the meal, which they had in a flowering arbour
on the edge of the Garonne. At two o'clock the three friends jumped
into a skiff and sailed up the river against the current. After a sharp
disagreement between Jacques and Edmond over whether or not to haul
the sail taut port and starboard, which almost made Jonathan seasick,
they drew alongside the *Hamburg*. Its engines were silent. The loading

could not be finished before nightfall, which meant they would not be sailing until the next morning.

It was all so ridiculous that if Jonathan had not had his trunk on board he would instantly have abandoned the exasperating ship. Jacques swore he would not allow the deck of the *Hamburg* out of his sight. Even so, Edmond succeeded in coaxing them ashore again for dinner. At nine o'clock, with earnest farewells and handshakes the two young men took leave of Edmond who said, laughing, that he hoped to see them again before the start of their impossible voyage.

It was a very dark night. Jacques and Jonathan walked down to the quayside at the far end of the Quinconces Esplanade. They could very well have walked down it as far as the Bacalan wharf but, fearing they would find no means of getting aboard from there, they chose instead to hail a boat. The boatman took some persuading, since it meant going back up the incoming tide. In the end, tempted by the large sum of three francs and fifty centimes, he decided to try his luck with the help of his twelve-year-old son. Seizing the oars, he rowed in a straight line towards the Bastide, so as to benefit from the backwash and drift downstream more easily. The crossing was difficult, however; the current was so strong, the boat scarcely seemed to advance. After an hour it had covered only half the distance, so Jacques removed his coat, took the boy's oar, and rowed vigorously.

Added to exhaustion was the difficulty of finding the *Hamburg*. How would they recognize it in the dark among so many ships? Jacques had tried to memorize its location, but he had not counted on having to find it at night. For an hour the boat drifted haphazardly, until the exhausted boatman began to talk about giving up and returning to the quayside.

'That would really be the last straw,' Jonathan said, deeply discouraged. 'What d'you bet we don't find the ship and it sails without us? We'll have spent seventeen days in Bordeaux for nothing.'

Jacques started, gritting his teeth and squinting into the night as the boat squeezed between the quayside and a schooner moored a few fathoms off. Jonathan, who was standing on his bench, was suddenly grabbed around the neck. He cried out as he fell over backwards with his legs in the air. The culprit was the schooner's mooring cable.

'Serves you right,' Jacques growled. He was becoming fierce.

Just then, he thought he recognized the light gleam given off by a gilded clipper bow. The dark mass ahead recalled the long slender profile of the *Hamburg*. He asked the boatman to head in that direction and was soon certain he was right. At last, after a two-hour search and with his faithful friend in tow, he climbed aboard and went to sleep with that small spark of undying hope still glowing.

Next day found the *Hamburg* steaming down on the ebb tide towards the estuary and the sea.

Proudly, Jacques watched the riverbank slip by. Scornfully, he waved goodbye to the Bec d'Ambès, to Pauillac and to Blaye. Even Jonathan smiled as he breathed in the invigorating morning air.

'We're on our way to Scotland!' cried Jacques.

'We're on our way somewhere!' said Jonathan.

Nothing special happened, except that the young composer had to act as interpreter between the captain and the pilot to help them settle the bill for the latter's services in Bordeaux harbour. It was a difficult exercise and coughing up this unfamiliar English left him in a heavy sweat.

At the mouth of the river a launch drew alongside. (p. 46)

At the mouth of the river a launch drew alongside. The bad-tempered river pilot's duties were completed and he was replaced by a second pilot whose task was to take the ship out to sea. The first one departed in the ship's boat as the second came aboard, the launch being towed by the *Hamburg*. There was a further delay as the captain completed formalities with a government sloop which acted as a guardship. At last the steamer rounded the Tour de Cordouan and its prow plunged into the billows of the Atlantic.

12

A night on the open sea

CAPTAIN SPEEDY WAS NOT yet in command of his ship. Like his predecessor, the second pilot did not understand a word of English. This may seem ridiculous, considering the number of British ships that call at the port of Bordeaux, yet it was so.

Moreover, no sooner had the pilot set foot on deck than his one thought was to leave ship as soon as possible. Night was falling and he did not want to have to return to shore in the dark. The steamer scudded rapidly between the red buoys that marked the mouth of the Gironde. The pilot was due to hand over to the captain after the last buoy and, looking through his field glasses, he tried to persuade him that it was already in sight. The captain trained his own glasses in the same direction and shook his head.

'No,' he said.

'What do you mean: no?' the pilot said, pointing out an invisible dot on the horizon. 'Don't you understand?'

The captain paced up and down the bridge without listening.

The pilot turned to Jonathan. 'If you please, sir, would you explain to him that my duties are over? The last buoy is perfectly visible over there, just a few cable lengths to leeward.'

'I can't see anything,' Jonathan said.

'Nor can I,' Jacques said, springing up to the first ratlines of the forestay. 'No buoy ahoy!'

'How very odd,' the pilot said.

The truth is: no-one else could see any sign of a buoy. The pilot alone pointed it out, with his southern self-assurance, repeatedly challenging the captain who refused to accept his questionable assertion. The pilot swore under his breath, calling him a hound, a John Bull, a Scottish mole – to no effect. They had been arguing for an hour when the buoy finally appeared. The pilot settled with the captain and jumped into his launch, which the *Hamburg* had been towing. The ship passed to the sole

command of Captain Speedy, who stood out to sea to weather the cape
of Brittany.

The sea was splendid and the *Hamburg* steamed ahead with a swift, easy
motion and almost no pitch. The foresail, spanker, topsail and jibs were
all spread easterly to steady the ship on the waves. Jonathan felt relaxed
and Jacques was as happy as could be. Around ten o'clock they withdrew
to their cabin and fell asleep in their drawer-like berths. Jacques got up
twice to enjoy the magic of a night at sea. He was so eager and receptive

The Hamburg *steamed ahead with a swift, easy motion and almost no pitch. (p. 48)*

he responded keenly to everything. The captain and his chief officer, a
burly fellow from Liverpool, took the watch in turns. Their brisk steps
rang on the bridge. From time to time they joined the helmsman to
study the compass, which was illuminated from within by a light, and to
check the ship's bearings. Then, with their hands in their pockets and a
pipe stuck between their lips, they resumed their round, unconcerned
by the whistling wind and the driving sheets of foam that whipped their
faces. A few sailors huddled motionless in the darkness fore and aft,
leaning on the rails, or lying on coils of cable, and a kind of stillness
seemed to hover amid the groaning of engines and the flutter of sails.

The magnificent sunrise reminded Jacques of descriptions by
Chateaubriand.[1]

'And now it's time to greet the captain,' he said.

'I'll do it for both of us, if you like,' Jonathan said.

'No need. I can manage. I've already picked up a few words.'

'As you wish,' Jonathan said. And he went off to speak to the first officer, who told him the ship was abreast of Brittany, off Belle-Ile.

Jacques approached the captain.

'*Good mourning,*' he said, giving him a hearty nautical handshake. '*Good mourning, captain.*'

The captain raised his head and said something which Jacques took to mean 'I'm fine, and how are you?' Delighted with his success, he moved on to the chief officer and repeated:

'*Good mourning, master.*'

The man started and gave him an odd look. Jacques was thrilled. He decided he had a great aptitude for English and went off in search of food.

Here is what the captain served his passengers for five shillings a day each. First of all, at eight in the morning, tea and buttered toast; at ten, luncheon with meat; at three, dinner with soup, meat and fruit pies; and finally, at seven in the evening, tea with Cheshire cheese.

This diet suited the two Parisians. They found the meat excellent. It was usually pork or beef, roasted in the English manner. The ham came from York and the tasty slices revived their stomachs. The vegetables were boiled without salt and served plain, thus replacing bread, which could not compare with Irish potatoes.

Water was the only drink served. The English hardly drink at all during meals, while Americans, who are more civilized, do not drink at all. Captain Speedy and his chief officer were certainly remarkably sober on board, although they did not hesitate to share a few good bottles of Bordeaux, which were a present from Edmond. At dinner, a huge tureen invariably appeared, brimming with a tasty soup in which huge pieces of meat and large chunks of vegetables mingled with pearl barley. The inevitable pie concealed creamy plums within its moist, golden casing. And when the dessert came round, the table groaned under the weight of the impressive cheese which grew steadily darker and more pungent.

All this was neatly served by the *waiter* in large china dishes under covers of British steel stamped with the ship's Dundee crest. Conversation never flagged and grew more lively as the gin and whisky flowed.

Jacques insisted on speaking English and the mistakes he regularly made brought tears of laughter to the eyes of the captain and the chief officer, while Jonathan did his best to explain the reason for their helpless mirth. Even when Jacques was lucky enough to hit on the right word, he pronounced it wrongly and created wonderful misunderstandings. Thus when at dinner, he addressed the captain in his own particular style:

'*Give me some bride.*'

Speedy burst out laughing.

49

'Do you realize what you've just asked for?' Jonathan said.

'Bread, of course.'

'No, you've just asked for a bride.'

'But I thought that *bride* –'

'*Bread*! You keep saying *bride*!'

'That's the problem,' Jacques said. 'Basically, all languages are alike. It's just the pronunciation that complicates things!'

Note

[1] such as the opening description of sunrise in *René*.

13

Problems with pronunciation

DURING THE DAY, the captain had cushions brought to the bridge for his guests who lazed there, smoking, talking, watching the long shadows of the clouds skimming over the waves and following the ship's course on the navigation charts. By Tuesday evening, the *Hamburg* was abeam of the Ouessant Islands, where it encountered a large school of porpoises.[1] Although mere sea-pigs, they are extremely graceful in their own watery element. Swimming at a fantastic speed, they overtook the *Hamburg*, leaping round it and splashing its sides with their powerful tails. This unexpected show lasted well over an hour, until nightfall, when the wind blew fresh and the captain had the topsail reefed. The sea was strong and heavy, with a choppy swell; the tow of the Channel current could be felt. Jonathan, however, faced the roll with the weathered equanimity of an old sea-dog.

During the night the sea grew heavier and the whole ship creaked under the combined onslaught of wind and wave. Jonathan had been sleeping for some time when around two in the morning Jacques woke him up to drag him on deck.

'Come on! We're travelling to gather impressions, aren't we?' he said. 'Let's go up.' And he persuaded him to follow.

The sky was covered with heavy black clouds and it was so dark the passengers could scarcely make out stem from stern. The tops of the masts were lost in the mist and the slackened sails flapped against the yards. Inside the wheelhouse, a light invisible to all except the helmsman[2] fell directly on the copper trimmings of the wheel. This circle of light twinkling in the heavy darkness created an eerie effect: the ship seemed to be guided by some supernatural hand, by means of this luminous wheel whose spokes and rim seemed ablaze.

'Isn't it all rather splendid?' Jacques said.

'Splendid,' echoed Jonathan, returning to his berth.

A tramping of feet woke them in the morning. The decks were being hosed down and swabbed. Special pumps operated by the ship's engine sent torrents of water in all directions and the pressure of the jets was such that all the dirt soon vanished overboard.

The *Hamburg* was admirably equipped. It had a special machine which operated a swivelling crane fastened to the deck. Being steam-operated, the loading and unloading of cargo could take place with British speed and efficiency.

When the captain arrived on deck, he was once again greeted by Jacques's '*Good mourning*', which made the man shudder.

The sight of the English coastline set his thoughts on a new tack. (p. 52)

Jacques was baffled. 'He doesn't seem to appreciate my greeting,' he thought. 'I know the British are eccentric, but still –'

The sight of the English coastline ahead set his thoughts on a new tack. Land's End – England's Cape Finisterre – reared up its sheer cliffs which the *Hamburg* skirted so closely that every single jagged detail was visible. Here was the extreme tip of ancient Cornwall, a hard barren land of thick mists whose shores are frequently battered by gales. A crudely constructed lighthouse rose from a lonely rock, with gentle waves lapping peacefully at its base. The sky was heavy, with that grey tint which often turns to fog over damp England. The Scilly Isles were soon left to leeward and the ship headed north in search of the entrance to St George's Channel.

After swabbing down the decks and getting through sundry morning chores, the crew did not have much to do. The sailors did not, however, apply to themselves that urge for cleanliness that made them so finicky about their ship, and no pump in the world could have scrubbed them clean. Never did a dirtier, grimier, tarrier bunch tread the deck of a merchant ship. A quiet, docile lot, they disappeared during the greater part of the day to their quarters aft, taking little notice of the two Frenchmen. At mealtimes they appeared with kettles of all sizes and shapes, but all invariably dirty and battered, which they filled with boiling water to make tea, that indispensable beverage of the British of all classes. It helped to wash down the chunk of dry bread rubbed with raw onion which was these sailors' staple diet. They had to pay for their own food and perhaps they had only their own carefulness to blame for this meagre, inadequate fare.

starboard

By the evening, the entrance of the Bristol channel had disappeared to port[3] and once again the travellers lost sight of dry land. They had settled into a seafaring routine, growing each day more keenly attached to this new way of life. Jonathan spoke a lot to the captain and the chief officer to improve his English, though he found it difficult to understand their replies, which were mixed with dialect. Scots is a mixture of three different dialects: English, Anglo-Saxon and Erse or Gaelic, which is also the language spoken in Lower Brittany. Speaking to these men was hard work and brought on a few headaches.

The Wednesday night was uneventful. After rounding the tip of Wales windward of the Pembroke coast, the *Hamburg* sailed into the dull heavy waters of St George's Channel.

'*Good mourning*, captain,' Jacques said, holding out his hand to the Scotsman, who looked irritated.

'*Good mourning! You are, sir, truly tedious!*'

'What's he got against me?' Jacques asked Jonathan, looking confused. His friend was laughing heartily. 'What's wrong with you all? When I say hello, he shrugs and you laugh your head off.'

'My dear Jacques, what on earth did you say to annoy him so much?'

'Well, the same as every morning: *good mourning.*'

'*Morning*, not *mourning!*' Jonathan exclaimed. 'Why, that's like asking the poor fellow 'when's your funeral?''

'Surely not?'

'I'm afraid so.'

'Ah well, in that case – good morning, captain!'

Notes

[1] Verne describes a ballet of porpoises in chapter 20 of *Les Tribulations d'un Chinois en Chine* ('The Tribulations of a Chinese Gentleman').

[2] Verne returns to this lighting effect in *Un capitaine de quinze ans* ('The Boy Captain') (I, 10).

[3] *to port*: provided of course, Jacques and Jonathan are standing aft: they are travelling backwards!

14

Arrival in Liverpool

AROUND FIVE O'CLOCK on Thursday morning they had cleared St George's Channel off Anglesey. The ship rounded the cape to westward¹ and scudded before the wind towards Liverpool, which the captain hoped to reach in the afternoon.

At six o'clock a handsome yacht looking like a pleasure boat drew alongside the *Hamburg*: it was in fact a cutter-rigged launch of the Liverpool company of pilots. A small boat approached and the pilot climbed aboard.

Jacques and Jonathan couldn't believe their eyes. Freshly shaved, meticulously gloved, dressed in black trousers and coat, with a silk hat on his head, a white collar at his neck and an overcoat slung casually over his arm, the Liverpool pilot displayed impeccable sartorial taste that would have impressed the most fastidious dandy. And all this before daybreak in the open sea! The man looked young and his regular features bore the stamp of British health and poise. Taking command of the ship, he studied the compass, gave the helmsman his bearings and placed himself at the service of Captain Speedy, who invited him to a meal a few hours later.

'That's an interesting foretaste of English customs,' Jacques told Jonathan.

'He looks much more distinguished than we do. He could be a Member of Parliament.'

'Especially if he gets drunk over dessert.'

But the pilot remained perfectly sober, even though he consumed the last bottles of Bordeaux.

Returning to the bridge, Jacques noticed a large paddle-steamer speeding past on opposite tacks. Its paddle-boxes were emblazoned in polished copper with the three legs of the Sicilian coat of arms. Swifter than the *Hamburg*, it plied between Liverpool and the Isle of Man.

By then the sea was crowded with a great number of tugs built on the same model, each with its jackstaff and tall funnel, looking out for incoming ships bound for Liverpool from all over the world.

A Royal Navy sloop was taking soundings in the channels at the entrance to the Mersey, the deep, wide river that forms Liverpool harbour. The entrance to the port is impressive. On the left stands a row of huge buildings displaying the English passion for order, and a great many lights illuminate this part of the coast. To the right lies the point of Birkenhead, the cannon of its fort commanding the whole roadstead. Liverpool harbour occupies the whole estuary, and from the Irish sea, it stretches inland along the river for some seven or eight miles.

The *Hamburg* was already steaming past granite walls where large black lettering spelled out the names of Liverpool's immense docks, unequalled in the whole world. On reaching Victoria Tower, which guards the main harbour entrance, the ship dropped anchor in the middle of the river: the state of the tide made it impossible to enter the docks.

Jacques and Jonathan did not have enough eyes to take in the thousand details of the scene. It was about two in the afternoon and since they could not disembark before the customs' inspection, they decided to have their meal on board so as not to lose time. They went down to the saloon, where they dined in the company of Captain Speedy, the first officer and the customs officer, a very pleasant man who bore no external signs of his trade. He promised to clear their luggage swiftly, without delving too deeply into their trunks. Over the dessert, Jacques toasted the Scottish captain and his ship. Hearty thanks and equally hearty handshakes were exchanged, and their luggage was lowered to a boat that had been waiting alongside for some time. At last the two young men left the *Hamburg*, each with a tight feeling in his heart, sad to leave a ship they would never see again.

The boat took them to a flight of stone steps cut in the quayside. Slimy, slippery steps had been laid bare by the low tide and made it difficult to reach dry land. There was anxiety over the fate of the trunks as they wobbled on a porter's shoulders. Once on the quayside, Jonathan managed to make their guide understand that they wanted a carriage. They crossed the docks and at a harbour entrance on the far side found a cab. They climbed in, handed the porter a few coins without being quite sure of their value and asked to be driven to a hotel near the station from which the Edinburgh trains left. Their cabby left them in front of the Queen's Hotel on St George's Place.

Paying the fare was the next task, a difficult one for people unused to the going rates and to the value of the local currency. Jonathan, who held the purse-strings, floundered among the copper and silver coins, crowns, half-crowns, two-shilling pieces, sixpences, fourpences, threepence and pennies with worn heads and tails that gave no clue whatsoever as to their value. Silver and copper coins are worth much less in England than in France. At the current rate, sixpence may be considered the equivalent of the fifty-centime coin while the shilling, which is worth one franc twenty-five centimes, roughly corresponds to the one-franc coin. This proportion is regular throughout, with the sovereign, which is worth twenty-five francs, used like the French louis.[2]

After much fumbling and hesitating, Jonathan parted with a half-crown, which is a little over three francs. It was a lot for a ten-minute ride.

As they settled down in their room at the Queen's Hotel, Jacques said: 'Well, here we are in England at last!'

'Yes, but we're still far from Scotland, which is our goal!'

'Give us time to breathe! We've only just arrived.'

'We'll have to do some fast breathing. There isn't a minute to be lost. It's twenty-four days since we left Nantes and we must be back in Paris at the beginning of September. You can see how little time we have left to reach Edinburgh, visit a few lakes and mountains, return to London and cross the Channel. It's ridiculous! All because of a late ship.'

'Don't be hard on the *Hamburg*, Jonathan. She's a good ship and sails well.'

'Once she's on her way. But, without wishing to offend her, she wasn't exactly quick off her mark. Anyhow, its no use crying over spilt milk. We must draw up our plan of campaign.'

'Very well.'

'We should, one, post the letters we wrote on board; two, inquire about the times of trains to Edinburgh; three, call on Mr Kennedy on behalf of my brother and, four, visit Liverpool this evening, tonight and tomorrow morning.'

'Fine. Let's go.'

'The snag is, which way?'

'No idea,' Jacques said. 'That's what's so attractive about this journey. As one of the deputies said during the Convention, you never travel so far as when you don't know where you're going.'

'So long as we're back in time, I've no objection. Let's go.'

Notes

[1] *The ship rounded the cape to westward:* one would have expected *to eastward,* but in this 'backwards' journey west has become east – just as south replaces north in *Voyage au centre de la Terre* ('Journey to the Centre of the Earth').

[2] First issued in 1640, during the reign of Louis XIII, the louis, or louis d'or was a gold coin worth first ten, then twenty-four francs. After the French Revolution it was replaced by a twenty-franc coin which was still popularly called the louis.

15

Exploring Liverpool

THEIR FIRST VISIT was to the station of the Caledonian Railways, which was on the same square as their hotel. The train for Edinburgh was due to leave on the following afternoon at two, but this they learnt only with some difficulty. Although the public is free to come and go unhindered in English railway stations, even on the platforms, there are few officials to inform them. It took Jonathan's sharpest wits to interpret a timetable that was far from clear.

Posting letters caused them some embarrassment because Jonathan did not know how to ask for postage stamps in English. In the end a chemist sold them some, and taught them the word for *timbres-poste*. Having overcome that problem, they were able to call on Mr Joe Kennedy, Custom House Street.

That worthy tradesman received them affably in dark offices where gas lamps had to be lit by four in the afternoon. The street itself was gloomy enough, with its tall houses of smoke-blackened yellow brick and grimy windows adorned with small mobile pulleys. As for Mr Kennedy, he was a formidable example of the English shipowner, with his powerful head framed with bushy sideboards and his ruddy, not to say glowing, complexion. He solemnly placed himself at the young men's disposal and invited them to a picnic that very evening. Eager to discover English customs as soon as possible, they accepted readily. The meeting was fixed for nine o'clock at the Bull and Mouth Inn, with detailed explanations of how to get there.

To fill the hours until dinnertime, Jacques and Jonathan headed for the docks down narrow, muddy streets that flaunted the misery of England with hideous lavishness. Most of the women wore hats – but hats that defied description: having first bloomed on the golden locks of prosperous ladies, then faded on the buns of chambermaids or shopgirls, they had finally come to rot, literally, on the heads of the most pitiful creatures on Earth. Discoloured ribbons and flowers – their

Muddy streets flaunted the misery of England with hideous lavishness. (p. 59)

names lost even to experts in artificial botany – stuck to these hats somehow, held in place by that dank, grimy blend of fog and coal-dust so typical of England.

Clad in thin rags, the poor women walked barefoot in slimy black mud. Their dragging gait, their bent shoulders and their poverty-scarred cheeks summed up the utter hopelessness of industrial city-dwellers. In countless workshops, where the police carry out fewer controls than in France, tasks are set beyond human strength. Labour is vilely cheap. In countless sordid rooms, women toil fifteen hours a day, often with no dresses, petticoats or blouses to wear, wrapped only in rags. Some are said to have spent years in this way without ever being allowed to go out.

The streets where this working class rotted swarmed with children. It was impossible to move a step without jostling a group of yelling, half-naked urchins wallowing in the quagmire. They spoke English, of course, as was to be expected; yet Jacques was amazed by this and, absurdly, could not get used to it.

Overall, the atmosphere was one of total freedom. Policemen seemed to intervene in people's affairs only when asked to do so. There appeared to be fewer disputes than in France, and certainly less noise.

Here and there this freedom of movement degenerated into licentiousness and the strangest professions were carried out in the open, apparently without outraging English prudery.

'Prudery in words alone,' Jacques commented.

The district adjoining the docks was bustling with activity. Every street corner had its public house selling ale and spirits. Drinks were gulped down at the bar, with ale and port[1] arriving in glasses full to the brim. Jacques found the former excellent but decided to leave the latter to the porters, whose inclination for the drink at a time when no-one else

The streets where this working class rotted swarmed with children. (p. 60)

favoured it is said to account for its name. As for gin, brandy, whisky, rum toddy (a kind of grog), mint julep and cocktails (a spicy mixture that brought tears to the drinkers' eyes), Jacques refused to have anything to do with them.

The true magnitude of Liverpool, which until then had seemed a town like any other, became apparent at the harbour. Its wet docks represent a Herculean achievement that is impossible to visualize, spreading out, double, triple even, over more than a league. How they open one into

Drinks were gulped down at the bar. (p. 61)

the next is such a mystery that not even Ariadne's thread could guide a stranger out of such a liquid labyrinth. Ships are berthed so close that their mass blots out the water, ships of all sizes, shapes and shores: American clippers built on a huge scale, whose superstructures could hold a nation; stout Dutch galliots, invariably spruced and bright under their tarry varnish; slender steamers whose long ornate prows curve along the quaysides; three-masters, whose tonnage would put first-class frigates in the shade; sailing lists pinned to colourful boards at the sterns of a thousand ships; delightful poetic names embossed in gold letters, names borrowed from the legendary lands of India and the East Indies, from Africa's burning shores, the gulfs, straits and rivers of America and the South Seas; flags from all the globe's nations floating in the mist, challenging the uniform grey with their gaudy colours. In the holds, there are mounds of bales bursting with coffee, sugar, cotton, stacks of logwood and mahogany, samples of every single colonial produce, all filling the air with exotic aromas; an army of workers, most of them wearing black hats and large aprons fastened round their waists; coaches sliding along rails that crisscross in intricate loops; weird machinery designed for specific tasks – crabs, cranes, a whole mechanical menagerie in perpetual motion, lifting bales, sacks and crates all bulging with goods; and, in the very heart of this bustling anthill, the whistling of steam, the chug and rattle of tramp steamers, the screeching of chains, the hammering of caulkers against a ship's side, coaches thundering on swing-bridges, hooves clattering on plates of metal, the swish of water as

62

An army of workers, most of them wearing black hats and large aprons fastened round their waists. (p. 62)

ships bump against each other, and the wind whistling through the forest of masts to the muffled breathing of the incoming tide – such are the sights and sounds of these docks that contain a whole sea, such the activity, the rhythm, the sounds – in a word, the life – of the port of Liverpool.[2]

Notes

[1] This is *porto*, in the French: but did Verne mean porter?
[2] The whole description of Liverpool harbour was closely reworked and polished by Verne.

16

Strange English customs

AFTER A LONG WALK, which enabled the two friends to discover all these extraordinary sights without pausing to dwell on details, they reached a floating wharf on iron rafts which rose and fell with the tide, making it easier to reach and leave the Birkenhead ferries. The steamboats used for this crossing are equipped with rudders at both the helm and the bow: by using them alternately, the ferryman does not need to manoeuvre and thus saves precious minutes. The boats are always crowded with passengers and, although the crossing lasts barely ten minutes, every ferry is equipped with a compass, since fog is common on the river and can blot out the opposite shore.

With Jonathan in tow, Jacques jumped into one, and for the modest price of one penny they crossed over to Birkenhead. People of all social ranks crowded on the deck. There was no distinction between first-class and second-class seats. Tradesmen, fishwives and workers sat side by side without bothering about their neighbours: any distinction would have wounded the British sense of equality. Jonathan found himself sitting next to a poor girl with an empty basket who was returning to Birkenhead at the end of her day's work. The sweet, pretty features of her worn face were moving to behold; her head sunk on her bosom, her crossed bare feet, the apathy of her careless posture, all betrayed a hopeless resignation. Jonathan entered into conversation with the poor girl and learned that her mother had died on giving birth to a fifth child and that her father had abandoned the distressed family. Being the eldest sister, she had four children to bring up. Until now she had succeeded not in feeding them, but in delaying the time when they would starve to death. She told Jonathan of her sufferings with dry eyes where tears had long since ceased to flow. Nothing was more depressing than this story, which is the fate of so many Liverpool workers. Jonathan gave the girl a few coins and her only surprise seemed to be that a foreigner should take an interest in her. On reaching the landing-stage, she soon disappeared, without looking back. What a grim fate awaited that girl! A life of misery if she concentrated on doing her duty, of shame if she heeded the advice of her dangerous charms.

Jacques and Jonathan returned to the docks; it was almost time for their appointment with Joe Kennedy. They headed for the tavern in thick fog through which the gas lamps shone dimly. With nightfall, the shops and stalls closed, business activity ceased and the streets were left in almost total darkness.

Mr Kennedy's two guests were greeted with cold courtesy. Being unaccustomed to English manners, this startled them and put them on the defensive. The company consisted of a dozen peaceful-looking fellows who seemed to make it a duty to meet for supper. Mr Kennedy introduced the two strangers to one of his friends, Sir John Sinclair,[1] in the manner described so often by Cooper and sounding just like Captain Truck in *Homeward Bound*:

'Mr Sinclair, Mr Lavaret. Mr Lavaret, Sir John Sinclair. Mr Sinclair, Mr Savournon. Mr Savournon, Sir John Sinclair.'

With this, the three men had been introduced.

The meal was a picnic, with each of those present paying his share, but in England even informal gatherings require a chairman and vice-chairman. A chairman had to be chosen, therefore, and Sir John Sinclair was elected. With a stiff bow, he took the place of honour. The vice-chairman, a heavy red lad with a butcher's shoulders, faced him across the table, while the two young Parisians chose to sit side by side.

'What a lot of fuss to eat plain roast beef and ham and eggs,' Jacques said.

'There's nothing really odd so far, but no-one's paying us any attention so let's just eat and watch.'

Inevitably, the meal consisted of tasty York ham and of a joint of beef carved from the side of a gigantic Devonshire ox. The guests swallowed huge pieces without drinking and scarcely pausing for breath. They ate using the left hand, spiking with their forks carefully combined slices of ham and beef which they covered with a thick layer of mustard. There were no napkins, so everyone wiped his lips on the tablecloth. Near-total silence reigned in the smoke-filled room. Waiters dressed in black came and went quietly, speaking in low voices.

Most of the meal took place in this way. Jacques was hoping that the drinks served with the dessert would inject some life into those stuffed shirts when an unexpected incident set the gathering on a very different course.

The vice-chairman took it into his head to leave the room. Grave as a judge, Sir John Sinclair asked to know the reason, but Mr Brindsley, the vice-chairman, did not answer and headed for the door.

'Mr Brindsley,' the chairman said imperiously, 'you may not leave without first obtaining my consent.'

'And why should I do that?'

'Because I am in the chair, and any such request must be made to me.'

'I'll be damned if I do,' the vice-chairman replied.

'You still insist on leaving?'

'I do.'

The other guests sat quietly awaiting the outcome of this discussion.

'Careful now,' Jacques said, 'we are about to have an example of English manners.'

As Mr Brindsley opened the door, Sir John Sinclair asked quietly:

'Mr Brindsley, would you be so kind as to remove your coat?'

'With pleasure. It will be fists, I presume?'

'As you can see.'

The table was immediately moved to one side to leave enough space for the pugilists. Used to such rituals, the waiters closed the doors carefully. Seconds came to assist the two champions who closed in, with one fist on the offensive, the other defensive.

'Dear me,' Jonathan murmured, 'this looks a bit ominous.'

'Don't worry. It's is just their way of brightening up the evening.'

Mr Kennedy warned his guests that a battle royal was looming. (p. 68)

A few sharp blows rang out. Some cracked on the arms when parried, others were soon mottling the boxers' faces. The onlookers passed comments and made bets on the outcome. This gave rise to heated discussions and to yells of 'hip! hip! hurray!' Hitherto placid spectators started getting worked up in a manner that boded no-one any good. This was when Mr Kennedy warned his French guests that a battle royal was looming in which they would have to use their fists.

'He can count me out,' Jonathan told Jacques. 'I've had enough of this. I don't want to lose an eye.'

'Not even for a first-hand knowledge of the English way of life?' Jacques said.

'Suit yourself. I'm off.'

'That's impossible, Jonathan. Why, we're French; and a Frenchman abroad represents France. We can't run away! And in any case, the door's shut.'

'I've got an idea. We'll get out of here if you do as I say.'

Everyone had joined in the fray. In English boxing slang, the chairman's conk was dented and the vice-chairman's spud-trap had a few broken teeth. The noise grew louder. Joe Kennedy had just received a terrible blow in one eye. Claret was flowing everywhere. Suddenly the lights went out. Jacques and Jonathan had found the gas taps and turned them off. Taking advantage of the dark, they fled, though not without receiving a couple of nasty blows that left them with a lasting impression of the power of the British fist.

Note

[1] Verne used the same name for the hero of *Le Rayon vert* ('The Green Ray').

17

A noisy nocturne

'AND NOW,' SAID JONATHAN, when they were safely in the street, 'let's get back to the hotel'.

'And fast, because I don't think those honourable gents will find our joke to their taste. Ruining everyone's evening in that way just isn't done!'

'We're unlikely to meet them again, since we're leaving tomorrow.'

'Don't we owe Mr Kennedy an after-dinner call?'

'My dear Jacques, you pay an after-dinner call only when you have digested your meal peacefully, which is not the case in this instance. So back to the hotel and let's forget about Messrs Kennedy, Brindsley and Sinclair. I'm anxious to get to Scotland and leave this dreadful land, which harmony and musical inspiration seem to have fled. I only hope I can catch up with them again in Fingal's kingdom.'

Hardly had Jonathan spoken than the cavatina from *Il Trovatore*, 'Quel suon, quelle preci solenni'[1] reached his ears. Some poor soul equipped with a cornet covered in a thick layer of verdigris was playing painstakingly on the corner of St George's Place.

'He'll poison himself blowing in that carbonated copper,' Jacques said.

'Especially if he insists on playing that wretched tune.'

Pursued by the uncouth music, the two tourists reached the Queen's Hotel. It was a luxury to slip into real beds at last, with big white curtains draped over four posts in medieval fashion – although the feel of the stiffly-starched cotton was unpleasant at first. Beds take up most of the space in English bedrooms, leaving barely enough to move around in: sometimes one has to open a window to pull on a sleeve. The washstands are tall, massive, and equipped with enormous china utensils. Low, small tables are set out for the luggage. Hotels of this kind provide basic comfort which contrasts sharply with the cotton curtains and the worn, patched carpets. And yet this was a relatively high-class establishment, considering the price of five shillings a night per person which was displayed on the notice-boards.

The travellers were so exhausted they soon fell asleep – to be awakened by screeches and yells below their windows. Five or six women, all fairly young, were quarrelling and exchanging blows on the square. This did not seem to worry anyone. No watchman thought of separating them. Doubtless the poor creatures were fighting for some belated passer-by and outbidding each other with tempting offers. One of the youngest was still a virgin – against her will to judge by her words – and she made a suggestion so startling that Latin itself, for all its verbal boldness, would not be brave enough to translate; even Greek would not dare attempt it.

This scene of street morality went on for some time. Cursing Liverpool's female populace, Jacques had just gone back to sleep when brass notes roused him once again. There was no keeping still, so he got up, opened the window and leaned out. A proper, well-dressed gentleman was playing a trombone in a cab, with the instrument's long slides poking out of the window. The music-loving Englishman was playing to himself as he drove round the square. His powerful lungs bellowed out – there is no other word – the *Trovatore's* 'Ricordati, ricordati'. And every time the cab came round and the trombone's bell faced Queen's Hotel, that dreadful 'Ricordati' burst forth in appalling notes.

'Again! We can't get away from that tiresome *Trovatore*,' Jonathan moaned.

'Played in the English mode too, with fifty horsepower.'

Exhaustion finally triumphed over noise; but at daybreak the young men jumped out of bed to visit other areas of the city. They entered St George's Hall, where they saw a gigantic organ with ninety stops and a steam-powered swell. They then continued as far as St Peter's and St Paul's, two attractive churches. Their walls seemed to be covered with a thick layer of soot, which suits England's square massive saxon architecture since it blots out many details. They walked past a school built in the Gothic style, crossed the quadrangle of the Stock Exchange, which features a large bronze group, and strolled along the quayside, past the impressive customs house. This took them to New Prince's Dock, from where the Leeds canal starts. They were eager for a second look at the gigantic docks, so they took an omnibus which followed the outer walls of the docks along a good distance. Sitting upstairs, they caught sight of good old Captain Speedy on a passing omnibus. They exchanged waves.

Around twelve o'clock, Jacques and Jonathan re-entered the hotel lobby. They were served a substantial meal, which consisted of cold meat,

They went to the Caledonian Railway. (p. 71).

beer, tea and toast – as bread prepared in this way is known in English – which was served in a silver rack. After doing justice to the meal they settled their bill, not forgetting what they called the *attendance*, meaning the attendants, and, followed by a porter who carried their luggage, they went to the Caledonian Railway.

English railway stations have few or no waiting-rooms. Departures are fixed at regular intervals, but fares vary with the speed of the trains. Ticket offices are open well before the time of departure, enabling passengers to choose their seats at leisure and stretch out in their compartments as soon as they wish. Wanting to prove that he could manage, Jacques walked over to the office and asked earnestly for '*Two tickets of second class, if you please, for Edinburgh*'.

All the English he knew had gone into that sentence and he proudly received two second-class tickets; the price, however, he left Jonathan to work out, since that was asking too much of his linguistic abilities. No-one asked them to register their luggage, which they took with them into their compartment, where they waited impatiently for an hour. At last, the engine whistled – much more elegantly than its French equivalent – and the train plunged into a tunnel a mile long.

Note
[1] Leonora sings this in Act IV, scene 1, during the well-known 'Miserere' which Verne referred to at the end of chapter 2.

18

The excellence of British railways

O NCE THROUGH THE TUNNEL, the train picked up speed: English railways are much faster than French ones. Their motion is easier and this is due as much to the quality and span of the suspension as to a less rigid design of the lines. In contrast, however, English railways are poorly supervised, without guards or signalling every half-mile. Trains pass and follow one another almost continually – hence the accidents people hardly worry about, not to mention those no-one worries about at all. The coroner turns up to satisfy himself that the victims died a violent death and there the matter rests. Business activities, the pressure of trade and a heavy demand are considered valid excuses for these trivial murders.

English trains are much faster than French ones. (p. 73)

It must be said however that there are fewer accidents than one might expect, considering the risks taken. The apparent carelessness of railway officials and drivers conceals a special instinct for great industrial ventures. The British are, with the Americans, the world's leading mechanics. They shrink from no hurdle and when a new idea occurs to them, think up the machine to carry it out. In short, where engineering is concerned, they can achieve anything. It is not surprising that during the Crimean War a serious company was set up, with substantial capital, to tender for the siege of Sebastopol, offering to take the town within an agreed period of time, past which it would pay millions in compensation for every day that elapsed. New machines would have been built to carry out this project, which would certainly have achieved a speedier result, with less loss of life, than traditional warfare. But could there be any glory in a war reduced to a company transaction? 'A dilemma indeed,' Jacques added after sharing the above reflections with his friend.

The train passed through Wigan and Preston – the latter owes its fame to Adam, who named a charming *opéra comique*[1] after the town. The railway line cut through the green Lancashire countryside. English meadows and farms[2] have a refreshing greenery all their own, which provides the eye with a new sensation of colour. Watered by several rivers, heated by thermal springs, the country is rich in produce of all kinds. Trade and industry flourish there and the country folk enjoy prosperity in their neat cottages.

The train stopped briefly at Lancaster, a city which suffered cruelly in the War of the Roses. Historic towns like Lancaster which prospered in the Middle Ages have declined, losing ground to manufacturing centres, and the old city is less industrial than its powerful neighbours, Liverpool and Manchester. Its 15 000 inhabitants cannot compete with the 200 000 of Liverpool, which had a population of only 7 000 at the beginning of the eighteenth century.

After Lancaster, Penrith; then Carlisle and, at last, the Scottish border. At every station Jacques went down onto the platform for a whiff of the local atmosphere and to try and work out the names of the various places. Usually he failed, because English stations are badly laid-out and crowded with huge notice-boards bearing white lettering on a blue background. Jacques was bewildered by the countless array of signs and, like La Fontaine's monkey, which mistook Piraeus for a man,[3] he ended up mistaking one of them for the name of the place. This happened in Carlisle where, returning to the compartment, he told Jonathan:

'This place is called *Ladies' Room*.'

'Idiot!' Jonathan exclaimed. When he had explained, Jacques leaned out, furious with himself, and concentrated on the fleeting sights. He knew that the Scottish border was not far, so he looked for mountains.

Map of Scotland by Malte-Brun. (See note p. 4)

Mountains! An exhilarating sight indeed when one has never seen anything higher than Montmartre. A few moments later, they reached a station and this time he did not make a mistake: Gretna Green, the first Scottish town.

Sweet Gretna Green, whose name sends a thrill through lovers' hearts! Delightful name that rounds off the last chapter of many a novel, giving way to real events! The fisherman and the innkeeper – and not merely the smith, as was long believed – were entitled by Scottish law to wed couples. From the humblest Cockney to Charles Ferdinand of Bourbon, the king of Sicily's brother, hundreds of couples, all equal before love, have exchanged vows before those impromptu magistrates. Such marriages still take place, even though the government has banned them since 1846. Gretna Green slipped past the speeding train like a memory of past loves.

The two travellers were breathing the air of old Caledonia at last.

Suddenly Jacques, who was still leaning out, excitedly exclaimed:

'There it is!'

'Eh, my good friend?'

'My very first mountain.'

'Indeed! May I borrow it? I promise to give it back!'

Having been lulled to sleep by the journey and the dark, the travellers awoke in the Scottish capital. (p. 77)

'Laugh at me if you like, but come and have a look. Can you see that vague shape on the horizon? That's a real mountain, with its head hidden in the clouds.'

And indeed the first undulations of the Skiddaw Hills came into view; the top of an isolated summit was hidden in the mist. As the railway line cut through the folds of the mountain range, the countryside changed completely. Abruptly and without transition, it took on a wild, rugged appearance. The valley narrowed into a deeper gorge and the train rushed along a precipitous track that clung to the cliff-face of those old rocks. The dizzy speed was almost supernatural and at each bend the train seemed about to throw itself into the ravine where the black waters of a torrent raged. Sharp crags, dreary heathland, total solitude replaced the green, lively English countryside. This was already the land of the Ferguses and the MacGregors.[4]

Jacques and Jonathan could not tear themselves away from this sight. After an hour, however, this first view of the Scottish Uplands gave way to the Lowlands. Night was falling fast and the young men fell back in their seats, silently absorbing these new sensations.

Around eleven o'clock the train stopped at Carstairs Junction, where one line branches off for Glasgow and the other goes on to Edinburgh. At midnight, having been lulled to sleep by the journey and the dark, the travellers awoke in the Scottish capital beneath a torrential rainstorm.

Notes

[1] *Le Brasseur de Preston* (c.1830) by Adolphe Charles Adam (1803–56).
[2] farms. MS: 'femmes' (women!).
[3] This is a reference to La Fontaine's fable 'Le Singe et le Dauphin' ('The Monkey and the Dolphin') (Book IV, 7).
[4] Rob Roy in Scott's novel, is known by his surname MacGregor to French readers; Fergus is Fergus MacIvor, in the same book.

19

Edinburgh, first impressions

A<small>T THE STATION</small> they hired a cab and, following the advice they
had been given, asked to be driven to Lambret's Hotel,[1] on
Princes Street.[2] The streets were wide but steep and poorly-lit.
Princes Street appeared, with a line of low houses to the left, the railings
of a large garden to the right and, lost in the darkness beyond, a mass of
tall buildings.

The visitors were greeted on their arrival by a Frenchman, Mr
Lambret, who ran the hotel. They were shown to two separate rooms
up the world's most illogical staircase – British staircases are apt to
lead one astray. The rooms were rather mean and recalled old provincial
hotels of the kind still found in towns like Amiens or Blois.

To the right, on an abrupt hill with splendid gardens at its base, stood Edinburgh Castle.
(p. 80)

After leaving their luggage in the rooms and the keys in the locks, as is the general custom, Jacques and Jonathan went down to a fine dining-room, where they were served supper: cold roast beef, ham and two pints of an excellent Scottish ale which frothed in silver mugs emblazoned with the arms of the city.

Jacques was ravenous. He had not had a bite since his lunch in Liverpool and he went on eating for much longer than Jonathan who was studying a huge map of Scotland on the wall. At about one in the morning, they returned to their rooms. Before going to bed, Jacques could not resist opening his window. It overlooked Princes Street. The rain poured down in the heavy darkness and all he could see was a great number of luminous dots twinkling at a great height across what seemed to be a vast open space. Puzzling over this phenomenon, he fell asleep.

Smoky old Edinburgh, Auld Reekie, *as the city is popularly called. (p. 81)*

The first ray of sunlight had him leaping out of bed and Jonathan knocking at his door. Jacques dashed onto the balcony. Princes Street stretched below, a broad and magnificent thoroughfare. To the right, on an abrupt hill with splendid gardens at its base, stood Edinburgh Castle. In front of him, huge ten-storey tenements, riddled with windows, towered over the railway station. The view encompassed the whole of the Old Town, perched on a high ridge which sloped away to the left. Above and beyond, a mountain reared its head against the horizon.

'Let's start by climbing that,' Jacques said, pointing to the mountain.

'No,' Jonathan said. 'Let's visit the citadel first. Then we'll try to find somewhere for lunch, before tackling that steep climb.'

Jacques gave in and they both set off. It looked like being a fine day.

Princes Street runs along a narrow valley between the Old Town and the New. No tributaries flow into it from the left and about halfway along the street passes the railway station and public gardens with magnificent lawns. A building a hundred and fifty feet high unfurls countless flowerings of flamboyant Gothic on its angles, cornices, pinnacle turrets and sharp spire. This is the Scott Monument. Sir Walter Scott is represented, seated in a pensive attitude, in the centre of the lower dais, under the keystone of an arched vault. Sculpted in white marble, this statue is well-known; the head is sensitive and intelligent. The monument, however, is far too high for its setting. It is decorated with a great number of other statues representing many of Scott's endearing heroes and heroines. In the four alcoves on the lower level one can see (if not admire) the Lady of the Lake, Bonnie Prince Charlie, Meg Merrilies[3] and the Last Minstrel.

The street continues between Princes Street Gardens and, to the right, a line of low buildings mostly intended for travellers and variously called Queen's Hotel, Gibb's Royal Hotel, Caledonian Hotel, Campbell's North British Hotel.[4] The Royal Academy and the National Gallery, in a Greek and an Etruscan style respectively, stand with gardens on both sides. Although more or less successful on artistic grounds, these monuments are finished and carefully maintained, like all public buildings in England and Scotland. One finds no unfinished cornice, no provisional masonry that all too often overstays its planned time, no ugly scaffolding that rots away even before the work has reached completion.

Having reached St John's Church at the end of Princes Street, the young Frenchmen turned left up Lothian Road, past the Caledonian Railway station. Their aim was to walk round the rock on which the Castle perches like an eagle's eyrie. In former times, this hill constituted the whole of smoky old Edinburgh, *Auld Reekie*,[5] as the city is popularly called. The old town stretches in a straight line from the Castle to the Palace of Holyroodhouse, down the High Street and through the Canongate area, with two high bridges linking it to the hills which respectively house the New Town to the north and suburbs to the south. This hilly site is ideal for fine buildings and views. There is no shortage of either in Edinburgh, hence its name of Athens of the North. Proud of its university, colleges, schools of philosophy, poets and orators, Edinburgh lives up to this glorious name both physically and morally.

As they crossed the Grassmarket, Jacques pointed out to his friend the austere, craggy appearance of the old rock of green basalt which is crowned by the buildings of the Castle. Public executions used to take place there and Scott chose the site for the hanging of Captain Porteous, one of the most dramatic scenes in *The Heart of Midlothian*. Jacques, who had read this fine novel before leaving, impressed Jonathan with his knowledge. This was where the 'lockman', the public executioner, operated; he had the right to levy a small amount of flour from all the

Jacques had developed an archaeological passion for the old Tolbooth. (p. 82)

sacks displayed at the town market. It was nearby, in a narrow alley, that the ghastly incidents involving the strangler Burke took place.

The young men came out on the High Street near St Giles' Cathedral and Parliament House, but they were unable to muster much interest in either. St Giles' was in their opinion a rather heavy example of Anglo-Saxon Gothic, and Parliament House an insignificant building on the corner of a square with a poor equestrian statue of Charles II in the centre.

On reading *The Heart of Midlothian*, Jacques had developed an archaeological passion for the old Tolbooth, where poor Effie Deans was imprisoned and suffered so bitterly. He had studied that part of the novel carefully and intended to show off his knowledge; by now, he reckoned, they should have reached the sinister prison. He looked around eagerly, but to his despair could see it nowhere. To comfort him, Jonathan suggested that they ask someone.

'Let's try in that bookshop.'

'Very well, but if the bookseller doesn't know, no-one else will. For this is the very spot where old Mistress Macleuchar had her laigh shop or cellar; this is where she spoke to the jolly Antiquary who fumed while waiting for the Queensferry Diligence, otherwise known as the Hawes Fly. Why, you can almost see the Laird of Monkbarns trotting up and down the Bow and the Canongate in search of some mutilated manuscript or of one of those small Elzevir editions which he took home triumphantly.'

While Jacques made this speech, Jonathan had entered the bookshop and come out again, having learned nothing. The bookseller had never heard of a novel called *Edinburgh Prison*.

'That's queer,' Jacques said. 'Are you sure he understood you?'

'Of course he did.'

It was only later that Jacques had an explanation. The novel, which French readers know under the title *La Prison d'Edimbourg*, was published in English under the name given to the old prison at the time when the story is set, *The Heart of Midlothian* – Midlothian being the county of which Edinburgh is the capital. As for the prison, it no longer exists, having been demolished in 1817. Owing to the kindness of an old friend, Robert Johnstone, who was then dean of the city's guild, Scott obtained permission to remove the gateway stones and the huge door locks, and use them to decorate the entrance of his kitchen-court at Abbotsford.

Notes

[1] Probably a misprint for 'Lambert's Hotel'.
[2] In Verne's original text – Prince's Street.
[3] Meg Merrilees: the gypsy in Scott's *Guy Mannering*.
[4] Campbell is the heroine's surname in *Le Rayon vert* ('The Green Ray').
[5] In Verne's original text – Auld Recky. Verne used this name again when describing Edinburgh in *Les Indes noires* ('Child of the Cavern'), chapter 17. Nell's visit in the company of Harry, Jack and James Starr is based on the wanderings of Jacques and Jonathan. In both cases, the characters climb Arthur's Seat and are always quoting Walter Scott.

20

A city of sharp contrasts

'WHAT WOULD MAKE ME really happy,' Jacques said as they walked down the High Street, 'would be to find a tavern at the sign of the Wallace Arms, the Three Cranes or the Southwark Mail. That would add a nice local flavour to our lunch, don't you think?'

'I've no objection,' Jonathan replied, 'provided we do get a meal, with or without an inn sign.'

Finding somewhere to eat in Edinburgh can be difficult unless one goes to an hotel. Unlike Paris, the city has no restaurants, and what few inns there are have no signs. By dint of persevering, however, our ravenous tourists discovered some kind of coffee-house outside the Tron Kirk[1] where for a modest sum they feasted on cold meat and Scottish ale, which they enjoyed. Jonathan would have liked a couple of fresh boiled

They headed towards the Palace of Holyrood. (p. 86)

eggs but could not make himself understood, not knowing the English for *à la coque*.

After their substantial meal, Jacques mentioned his intention of climbing the mountain he had seen from the hotel window – and Jonathan had to go along. They headed towards the Palace of Holyrood down the High Street, the popular thoroughfare which Scott describes so well in *The Abbot*, and crossed the junction of the North and South Bridges, with their gigantic arches linking the three hills of the city. At the southern end of this street one can see the university, built on the

The house of John Knox, the great reformer. (p. 86)

site of the house which the Earl of Bothwell blew up, along with Darnley's corpse. It is impossible to take a step in Edinburgh without encountering the living traces of Mary Queen of Scots or stepping into one of Scott's poignant ruins. Further down, the High Street becomes the Netherbow and runs past the house of John Knox, the great reformer, who alone of all men remained insensitive to the Scottish Queen's smiles – which is why he died a peaceful death in his own bed on 24 November, 1572. Netherbow then yields to the Canongate, that ancient street which once constituted the whole city.

The area that leads to the royal palace is one of utter misery. Naked children, barefoot women and girls dressed in rags, beggars with hats, jostle, pass, drag themselves along and slink past the tall tenements with their pinched, starved features. And yet, in the midst of that abject populace, in the foul, disease-ridden atmosphere, on the muddy paving and down those dark, dank, horrid lanes or closes which lead to revolting slums, slithering down stepless ramps toward the ravines on either side of the Canongate, one is gripped by the terrible poetry of old Scotland. For here it was that Waverley stayed on his first visit to Edinburgh; here a tailor cut for him that celebrated battle-tartan which the Widow Flockhart so admired. Here, no doubt, the rejoicing Highlanders fired their guns in the air after the Young Pretender's victory, and Flora MacIvor was almost hit by a wild bullet. Nothing can compare with the Canongate. Its idiosyncratic nature is unique; its shops, stalls, creaking signs on iron chains, its large eaves, the still-standing smithies of former hostelries, and the prison clock with its baleful face overhanging the street: all this gives the Canongate an appearance and an atmosphere that only the brush of Delacroix could capture.

In this street, as indeed elsewhere in the city, women seem to far outnumber men. This may be due to the fact that menservants are a tiny minority in Edinburgh, which swarms with servant girls and chambermaids who rush up and down the streets, wearing their mistresses' old hats.

The street widens as it approaches Holyroodhouse. It leads one past a hospital and the Canongate kirk – a Gothic building with its prominent graveyard but no style or character – and comes at last to a square beyond which rises the palace of Scotland's former kings and queens.

A big crowd had gathered in the middle of the square to admire a charming new fountain. It displayed the splendour of Renaissance Gothic and consequently lacked purity of style; yet its stonework seemed so delicate and so intricately sculpted, so refreshingly spontaneous, like a tropical flower that has blossomed in a single summer night.

Jacques and Jonathan walked down to the Palace of Holyrood, where guards still wear the traditional Scottish costume, a kilt of green cloth, a plaid, and a long-haired goatskin purse hanging over the thigh. As the two visitors did not have much time to spare, they contented themselves with admiring the four large crenellated towers which give the façade a medieval air. Except for the ruined chapel that raises its naked Gothic arches behind the palace, it is impossible to guess which parts of the building are new and which have been restored. Despite the dramatic events and heinous crimes that took place within those walls, despite the frightful memories of the love between Mary Queen of Scots and the unfortunate Rizzio, the old dwelling does not have a grim or gloomy appearance. On the contrary; it looks like a small pleasure-château whose owner has preserved its medieval character by some whim. Only a deposed king, like France's Charles X, could fail to enjoy total peace there, with no regrets for the past and no worries for the future.

'Holyrood! Holyrood!' Jacques exclaimed, quoting Victor Hugo's fine lines.[2] Then he added: 'Shall we climb that mountain now?'

'It looks a bit steep,' Jonathan said. 'Surely we should ask whether there's an easier way up.'

'Nonsense! I'm going straight up.'

He dashed across the Queen's Park,[3] which stretches to the right of the palace. A cavalry regiment was exercising there and the gleaming weapons and red uniforms created a bright splash in the landscape, where a few trees fringed the shores of a small loch or pond at the foot of the hills.

'Holyrood! Holyrood!' Jacques exclaimed, quoting Victor Hugo's fine lines. (p. 88)

Jacques could not help recalling the scenes from *Waverley*, set in that very place. Charles Edward's army had gathered there, with waving tartans, floating plumes, and unfurled banners bearing the rallying cries of the Clanronalds, MacFarlanes, the Tullibardines and the Gordons. In the midst of them all rose the standard of the Chevalier with the motto *Tandem Triumphans*, which he would soon live up to at the Battle of Prestonpans.[4]

To the right, violent explosions could be heard at regular intervals, with answering echoes from the cliffs of the mountain. A company of riflemen in dark uniforms were practising with precision weapons.

They crossed Victoria Drive, a magnificent circular drive for carriages that Walter Scott prided himself on having obtained for the city, thanks to a few lines in *The Heart of Midlothian* which compose a delightful picture of the paths that twist round the base of Salisbury Crags. These crags form the pedestal of Arthur's Seat, the very mountain Jacques had set out to climb. He refused to believe it was one thousand feet high: it seemed no more than three hundred to him. The unfamiliar Scottish scenery was to confuse his judgement more than once in this way. At last, with poor Jonathan lagging far behind, he reached the top of Arthur's Seat, covered in sweat, unable to breathe and missing heartbeats. He had sworn not to glance back before reaching the top, so he closed his eyes, turned to face the city and opened them again.

His amazed eyes had never seen a more splendid sight. Arthur's Seat raised its solitary head above the surrounding hills. The whole city was spread out below, with the modern districts and regular streets of the New Town contrasting with *Auld Reekie's* confused tangle of houses and crazy network of alleys. Two landmarks dominated the skyline, the Castle on its basalt rock, and Calton Hill, with the ruins of a Greek temple on its rounded summit. Splendid tree-lined avenues converged on the capital. To the north, an arm of the sea, the Firth of Forth, with the Port of Leith at its mouth, cut deeply inland. North of the Firth lay the harmonious coastline of the kingdom of Fife; to the east stretched the boundless expanse of sea which always looks blue and calm when viewed from such heights. A road as straight as the one to Piraeus linked this new Athens to the North Sea, as Charles Nodier observed.[5] The distant peak of Ben Lomond was visible to the west and below, to the right of Arthur's Seat, stretched out the beaches of Newhaven and Portobello, with their bathing resorts. No pen can do justice to this breathtaking scene. Jacques was silent, in the grip of the awe that is aroused by nature's sublime displays. Jonathan, who had caught up with him, shared his speechless admiration. They stood there, fascinated, breathing in the pungent draughts of the sea-breeze.

'Let's go down,' Jacques said at last, 'let's go or we'll never be able to tear ourselves away from this enchanted spot. Come on, Jonathan.'

They had taken the steepest way up to Arthur's Seat so they chose a more gradual path that wound down the far side. Laughing, rosy-cheeked girls were coming up, giggling and exclaiming 'Oh my legs, my poor legs'. Proud to understand what they were saying, Jonathan smiled at them pleasantly. On his way down the mountainside, he decided to go to Portobello for a swim so, with Jacques at his heels, he headed in that direction across open country. Half an hour later they had reached the coast.

Portobello is a cluster of houses along an attractive beach. Whence comes that Italian name in this land of hard Gaelic sounds? Jonathan attributed it to the presence at Mary's court of the musician Rizzio and his companions. There, on the yellow sands, the Frenchmen recognized the bathing-scenes that British prints have popularized. Many families spent the hottest hours of the day on the beach; while the children played, watched over by nannies and governesses, their mothers and attractive young misses disappeared into the sea. Men bathed about ten yards away from the women. Bathing cabins took them out beyond the first waves.

'British prudery, I suppose,' Jacques said. 'We don't segregate the sexes like this in France.'

'It's a great pity, a very great pity,' Jonathan said. 'But when in Rome . . .'

Each entered a cabin.

'Jonathan!' Jacques called out after a few moments, 'do you think you could ask the attendant for a bathing-suit?'

'It's very awkward. I don't know the word for *caleçon*.'

'What about using sign language?'

Jonathan called the attendant, on whom gesticulating produced no effect, as he explained to Jacques.

'What do you mean, he didn't understand?'

'I can't help it. He's really stupid.'

'What shall we do? We can't just – '

The words froze on Jacques's lips. Through the open cabin door he had just seen a splendid male bather, a British thoroughbred, emerge slowly and gracefully from the water, in the most perfect nakedness.

'Jonathan! Can you see what I see?'

To Jonathan's amazement, other bathers were following the first one out of the water, all equally unclad and just as oblivious of the ladies and girls on the shore.

The two young men hesitated no longer. They made a dash for the first breaker and dived in without a backwards look.

'So much for British prudery!' Jonathan said, shaking his wet hair.

'I suppose bathing-suits would be the shocking thing here.'

Having bathed in Arcachon only a few days earlier, they found the water cold; but they were understandably shy about returning to their cabins in such primitive attire. In the end, they emerged backwards from the bitter swell[6] at the risk of entertaining all the young ladies on the beach with their awkward posture and hasty retreat.

Notes

[1] In Verne's original text – Tron-church.

[2] 'Holyrood! Holyrood!' is a hemistich from Hugo's poem 'Le sept août mil huit cent vingt neuf' in *Les Rayons et les ombres, II*. It was in Holyrood that the Count of Artois (the future Charles X) and his court sought refuge during the French revolution and the reign of Napoleon.

[3] Verne wrote 'King's Park' under the influence of *Waverley*.

[4] *Tandem triumphans*: 'triumphant in the end'; Prestonpans, east of Edinburgh, site of Charles's victory over the English in 1745.

[5] See Charles Nodier's *Promenade de Dieppe aux montagnes d'Ecosse*, Paris, Barba 1821, pp 125–6, chapter 12 'Edimbourg'.

[6] *they emerged backwards from the bitter swell*: backwards *(à reculons)* is a humorous echo of the French title *Voyage à reculons*. Tocqueville noticed girls bathing naked on an Irish beach 'a short distance away from young men' and concluded that sexual modesty was a consequence of corrupted morals, since in Ireland 'very few illegitimate children are born'. *Voyages en Angleterre et en Irlande*, p 331 ('Journeys to England and Ireland').

21

The New Town

AFTER THEIR DELIGHTFUL bathe, they went to a nearby tavern – little more than a booth – for a glass of excellent ale which set them on their feet again. Shortly afterwards the omnibus that runs between Portobello and Edinburgh arrived, so they climbed on board and succeeded in finding two seats in the crowd packed into the top deck. Women, children, old folk, dogs – all were accepted on the swaying vehicle. Passengers were squeezed in every corner and only by some miracle did the coachman, a solemn man in a black coat and bowler hat, retain his balance on his seat. The omnibus drove round Calton Hill and down Regent Road past the new prison, a jumble of small constructions in Anglo-Saxon style built in terraces along a low hill, with crenellated walls, stone observation turrets, windows with huge bars and countless machicolations: it looked like a miniature medieval town, perfectly clean as if waxed and polished.

The omnibus stopped outside the theatre,[1] a building about which the least said the better, and almost opposite the structure which houses the city archives,[2] topped by a badly proportioned dome.

From there the young men walked back to Lambret's Hotel to study a plan of Edinburgh. Jonathan's brother had married the niece of a respected Scotsman, Mr B–, who lived in Edinburgh with his family. Jonathan's visit had been announced and the young man knew he would be made very welcome if he called on the family. By being received in this Scottish household, he hoped to learn more about local manners. He invited Jacques to accompany him and his friend accepted eagerly.

Mr B– lived in Inverleith Row, on the outskirts of the city. This meant crossing the New Town and its fine streets – called place, terrace, road, row or street, to the confusion of outsiders.

Jacques pestered Jonathan with questions about Mr B–. Still influenced by Walter Scott, he wondered whether he should address him

93

as Your Honour or My Lord and he expected to meet an old-time laird in national garb.

Walking up South St Andrew Street, they reached a square[3] in the centre of which stood a monument to Melville, its fluted column topped by a statue and recalling Trajan's Column in Rome. Most of Edinburgh's monuments are copies or reduced models – not always successful – of famous edifices of Ancient Greece and Italy. On one side of the square stands the Royal Bank of Scotland, not to be confused with the Bank of Scotland or the British Linen Bank, a building with Corinthian columns a few paces away, or the Exchange Bank of Scotland, a hybrid mixture of Greek and Roman embellishments, or with any of the other banks that crowd the streets of British cities.

George Street[1] runs parallel to Princes Street, from St Andrew Square to St George's Church. It is a magnificent street lined with insurance company offices, libraries, museums and churches, all with monumental ambitions. As the friends walked down the street, the bells of St Andrew's church chimed gaily. Jonathan jotted down the tune in his notebook; it

'Haven't you ever noticed something odd about the map of Scotland and England? It represents a woman out for a walk.' (p. 95)

94

was a succession of notes in diminished fifths, C, F, B, E, A, D, G, C. This combination produced an unusual peel which struck his musician's ear.

Other passers-by paid no attention to the chime. They were brisk, grave people, quite unlike the crowds in the Canongate. The women, all wearing broad-brimmed hats, walked firmly and stiffly, taking long British strides. Their clothes were generally tasteless and inelegant, with jarring colours and long bodices that lengthened the bust and flattened the waist almost out of existence.

As one of these ungraceful women strode by, Jacques asked Jonathan:

'Haven't you ever noticed something odd about the map of Scotland and England? It represents a woman out for a walk. The train of her dress, with its rumpled flounces, sweeps right down to the Atlantic. Her long bodice reaches down to the girdle of counties between the Irish Sea and the North Sea. She sticks out her behind and throws back her angular head, with the Firth of Forth giving her a huge mouth. And she wears a round hat from which locks spill like tousled, floating islands. If you look carefully, you'll see I'm right.'

Clyde

As he spoke, they walked by an appalling statue of George IV. Down Hanover Street they came to Queen Street Gardens, which is in fact a kind of elongated square. All these magnificent streets intersect at right angles and are wide and clean but almost deserted. The houses are not tall, consisting usually of a kitchen basement, a ground floor, first and second floors, and are normally occupied by a single family. Each façade has only three windows. The front door, which is never a double-door, is reached over a small bridge under a Greek portico[5] and as he walked past Jacques read out the names of the residents' professions: he was greatly amused by *surgeon, physician, sollicitor* and even more so by those he could not understand. One in particular sounded terribly forbidding, causing him to shudder every time he read it on a door: *upholsterer.*[6]

'Don't worry, it just means *tapissier*,' Jonathan said.

'And what right, pray, does a *tapissier* have to bear a frightful name like that?'

Notes

[1] The Theatre Royal, replaced by the GPO in 1861.
[2] Register House.
[3] St Andrew Square.
[4] George Street. MS: 'St George's Street'.
[5] *under a Greek portico* replaces: 'which spans the yard between the basement and the street; it is covered with a little roof supported on columns. There are no carriage entrances.' The original text was more accurate than the amended version.
[6] *surgeon, physician, sollicitor* (sic), *upholsterer* are all in English in Verne's original text.

22

The charms of Miss Amelia

STILL WALKING IN THE DIRECTION of Leith, they eventually reached an elegant avenue called Inverleith Row. Half a mile down they came to Mr B–'s house. It was an attractive residence, with a neat dainty look about it, and tall windows that thirsted for daylight and fresh air. Railings enclosed a small front garden. Jonathan rang and when a servant opened the door he asked in his best English for Mr B–. Followed by Jacques, he was led up a gleaming staircase covered with a narrow carpet to a first-floor drawing-room.

Two women sat there, intent on needlework. They were Mrs B– and her daughter Amelia, a very pleasant young lady whose liveliness, courtesy and grace contrasted with the more usual British stiffness. The young Parisians introduced themselves. The family had been expecting them to call and thanks to Miss Amelia everyone was soon acquainted. Mrs B– did not speak French, but her daughter did so perfectly, despite her Scottish accent, having spent some time in Nantes and Paris. Jacques was delighted to find someone with whom he could have a sustained conversation and he courted Miss Amelia assiduously.

The ladies sent for a tray with two glasses and two bottles, one of port, the other of sherry, which is the English name for Xeres. Port and sherry are obviously the stock-in-trade of British cellars, for those invigorating refreshments are produced and served wherever one goes. After a drink and a few biscuits Jacques and Jonathan requested the honour of being presented to Mr B–.

'My father isn't in at the moment,' Miss Amelia said, 'but if you are so kind as to stay for dinner, you'll meet him then.'

Jacques excused himself in his and his friend's name: he did not wish to impose upon the family's hospitality, even though this was Scotland.

'Not at all,' the young lady replied. 'It will be a very simple dinner, but since Mr Savournon is a musician and I adore music, we can spend the evening at the organ and the piano.'

Amelia, a very pleasant young lady whose liveliness, courtesy and grace contrasted with the more usual British stiffness. (p. 97)

'In that case, since tomorrow is Sunday, and provided, of course, Mr and Mrs B–'.

'Oh, no, not tomorrow,' Miss Amelia said. 'You'll be dining with us again, of course, but it's against our principles to have music on Sundays. This is a fast rule for Catholics and Protestants alike.'

Unable to resist such attractive persuasion, Jacques and Jonathan accepted the double invitation.

'I shall now fetch my hat and shawl,' Miss Amelia continued, 'and show you some of our local sights until dinner.' Followed by her mother, she left the room.

The two young Frenchmen agreed that she was a delightful Scottish lassie.

The drawing-room was big, light and designed to meet all British requirements in comfort. As everywhere in Britain, the tall windows opened vertically on a system of springs and counterweights that recalled the old sash windows, except that these were much lighter. The panes were framed with thin strips of iron and the light flowed in unhindered. By doing away with inward-opening windows, shutters with close, slender slats could be hung on the inside. The fireplace, of black marble, was tall and almost flush with the wall. Its hearth was designed for burning coal. A small plain clock stood between two bronze candlesticks which were attached to the mantelpiece and received gas through a hidden pipe to light their triple burners. Gas was similarly distributed to every corner of the room and to the ceiling chandelier, providing light in a convenient manner. Armchairs of various shapes with unmatched coverings offered tired visitors the most relaxing contours. There were none of France's fashions or usages; everything was less luxurious but more comfortable. A Broadwood grand piano

Jacques courted Miss Amelia assiduously. (p. 97)

and a fine organ completed the furniture and contributed to the room's special note of harmony.

As often happens in Scottish households, the convictions of the B– family were shared between the Catholic and Protestant faiths. Mr B– was a stern Protestant, whereas his wife and daughter were of the Catholic faith, which mellowed the rigidity of puritanism with the charm of its tolerance, sociability and poetry. Faithful to John Knox, Scottish Calvinists have carried to an extreme the rigour of religious practice, to the extent of breaking with the Episcopalian Church, which has kept a hierarchy of bishops and priests while tolerating Calvin's dogmas. In Scotland's Presbyterian church all ministers are absolutely equal: released from liturgical and extraneous duties, their mission is solely to interpret the Bible in a rational and individual manner. Jacques decided to take a closer look at the two religions coexisting in the B– household.

After a few minutes Miss Amelia reappeared alone and with that freedom the young women of Britain enjoy she led her two guests on a new outing – 'to the Botanic Gardens,' she announced, 'which are just down the road. As it's Saturday, the hothouse will still be open and you'll see some strange plants there.'

Jacques offered Miss Amelia his arm and she took it graciously. They were soon at the entrance of the Botanic Gardens. With its small, unassuming gate, it looked like a carefully-tended private property. The lawns were splendid, as usual in Britain, and people walked over them as freely as on the sanded paths. Miss Amelia led her guests to the hothouse, a large glass rotunda sheltering exotic plants from all over the world, with an iron gallery around the top of the dome offering a magnificent view of the whole city.

This delightful outing lasted about an hour amid the endless questions which Jacques asked about Scotland and Miss Amelia about France. Back in Inverleith Row, Miss B– led them across the street to Edinburgh's new cemetery[1], as if it was a pleasure ground and the most natural place on earth to visit.

It was indeed a lovely garden, with lawns and box shrub borders along the paths. The tombs were a pleasure to contemplate and in that cool shaded place they made one yearn to lie down there in eternal peace. In such a cemetery, death does not take on the funereal gloom of France's mausoleums and truncated columns: the tombs are like charming cottages where life flows past, leisurely and pleasant. This peculiar feeling moved Jacques and enabled to him to appreciate why, so simply and naturally, Miss Amelia had led them to this entrancing park.

Note
[1] Warriston Cemetery on Warriston Road, laid out in 1842.

23

A family gathering

ON RETURNING TO THE HOUSE, the visitors found Mr B–
and the Reverend Mr S–[1] in the drawing-room. Mr B– received
them with dignified warmth, greeting them in their mother
tongue which he spoke in a slow, measured fashion. With his quiet,
distinguished manners he seemed to be the best man in the world.
Jacques looked in vain for the Scottish plaid and kilt. Mr B– was simply
dressed in a black suit.

The Reverend Mr S–, a Catholic priest, seemed to be a regular visitor
to the house. With his gentle kindly features, his deep earnest gaze, his
modest and discreet manner, he was the epitome of a British clergyman.
What a difference from those Presbyterian ministers, half priests, half
merchants, speculators in the trade and salvation of souls, of whom
British missionaries to the colonies are the most repulsive breed.

Now the incumbent of a tiny parish in Fife, Mr S– had travelled
extensively in Europe. A visitor to Rome, Vienna and Paris, he displayed
sound knowledge of the continent and spoke French perfectly, without
trace of an accent.

Dinner was announced and they all went down to the dining-room on
the ground floor. On entering, Jacques was struck by its austere,
awesome appearance; it reminded him of one of those medieval halls
where solemn family meals took place, presided over by the father. A
near-religious atmosphere reigned in the room, emphasized by the dark
hangings and furniture.

Jonathan was placed between Mrs B– and the Reverend Mr S–, Jacques
to the right of Mrs B– and on Miss Amelia's left. Before sitting down,
everyone stood for a few moments, inwardly saying grace.

A soup was served, a mixture of meat and stock. Miss Amelia told the
French guests that this was the national *hotchpotch*, to which they
rendered all due honours. The family had, Mr B– told them, decided not
to modify their Scottish habits.

101

Jonathan thanked him gratefully. 'My friend has had many an imaginary meal with Scott's heroes, so at this very moment he can believe himself the guest of Fergus MacIvor Vich Ian Vohr.'

'Monsieur Jacques's only regret is that we are not dressed in Highland costume,' Miss Amelia said.

'If you travel a little northwards,' the Reverend Mr S– said, 'into the mountains, there, around the shores of our lochs and in the glens, you will find that the local inhabitants have preserved to this day traditions of bygone times, including the Scottish costume and sense of honour.'

'Surely you intend to visit the Highlands?' Mr B– said.

'This is something we wished to discuss with you,' Jacques said. 'I for my part couldn't leave Scotland without enjoying more of it.'

'How do you like our country?' Miss Amelia asked. 'I expect one of our frank, honest replies.'[2]

'It's a wonderful country,' Jacques said, 'and an extraordinary place to visit. Generally speaking, nothing is done, said, considered, heard or perceived as in France. Every single word, action and sight offers fresh reasons for wonder and meditation. Our impressions can only be superficial, of course, but we're thrilled with our visit. I for one have not found any of my dreams about old Caledonia exceed the reality.'

'I agree entirely,' Jonathan said, 'and I expect we'll be even more impressed if we go into the mountains.'

The Reverend Mr S– nodded. 'You are quite right. And nothing can be easier. If you care to visit me at my brother's castle at O–, in Fife, this will give you a starting-point for a most interesting tour. You will then discover for yourselves that nothing can uproot from a Scotsman's heart those three loves he professes: the love of his country, which he manifests with burning patriotism; the love of his clan, to which he is stubbornly loyal; and the love of his family, whose members he honours unto the ninth generation, cousins included. All this is a survival from the feudal system of the Middle Ages which I do not have the courage to fight. Gentlemen, will you visit me?'

'Oh, do accept,' Miss Amelia said. 'It's the loveliest castle in Scotland, with a magnificent park and Scottish hospitality at its best.'

'We can well believe you,' Jonathan said.

'My only regret is that my brother and sister-in-law won't be there to do you the honours of their home. But I shall do my best to replace them.'

'It's very kind of you,' Jacques said, 'but we are pressed for time. Would this be a long excursion?'

'It need not be. All you have to do is take a steamboat up the Firth of Forth which will leave you an hour from Oakley'.

'From there,' Mr B– continued, 'you can cut across to Glasgow through Stirling and return to Edinburgh by Loch Lomond, Loch Katrine and the mountains.'

'So that's settled,' Miss Amelia said. 'It's a splendid excursion no tourist fails to make. In two days you'll see marvellous landscapes. I will plan your journey in detail myself so that you waste no time and miss nothing.'

The two young men accepted and it was agreed they would start on Monday.

The following day being Sunday, Mr B– reminded them that he was at their disposal to show them around Edinburgh, 'before coming back here for dinner. We shall be leaving town ourselves on Monday, so we may not see you on your return from the lochs.'

Jacques and Jonathan thanked their host warmly and left it to him to decide everything for the best.

Notes

[1] Verne had originally given the priest a name, which he then crossed out, making it illegible. He refers to him as Reverend throughout, although this would not have been the style of a Catholic priest.

[2] MS: our frank, honest replies. 'none of your French hypocritical flattery.'

24

On Scottish cuisine

INNER TOOK PLACE AMID interesting conversation, with Jonathan showing off his best English. Large quarters of roast meat, including joints of beef, appeared under silver covers. Plain boiled unseasoned vegetables shared the diners' plates with slices of beef and ham. Jonathan was allotted a splendid Portuguese onion the size of his fist which he mastered only after a hard struggle and much grimacing, thus saving his honour. This was followed by *grouses*, a kind of partridge with a delicate flesh enhanced by a taste of wild heather. Sherry and port were periodically sipped from small glasses. Noting that this custom did not suit the young Parisian stomachs, Mr B– called for a few pints of a most pleasant *table-beer*. The inevitable tart appeared for the dessert, after which, to round off the meal, each guest proceeded to concoct a weird drink, with the Frenchmen imitating their host as best they could. In the bottom of a tall glass designed for this purpose, they put a few spoonfuls of tamarind jelly over which they poured boiling water and rum. The mixture was then stirred with a special, long spoon before being transferred to a small glass also designed for this ritual. They drank from the small glasses which had to be constantly replenished and emptied, causing Jacques concern for his none too solid head. Finally, the meal over, everyone said grace and returned to the drawing-room.

The Reverend Mr S– immediately took his leave since he had to return to Oakley that very evening. He reminded the Frenchmen of their promise to visit him there, entrusted Miss Amelia with the task of planning their route and their means of transport, and arranged to meet them on Monday at eleven o'clock on the Crombie Point jetty.

Despite the lavish meal, tea was due to be served two hours later, so Miss Amelia proposed another outing to pass the time until then. Enjoyment quashing exhaustion, Jacques and Jonathan accepted as if they had not already had a full day. So Mr and Mrs B–, Miss Amelia and their guests walked up Inverleith Row as far as Newhaven. Situated one mile from Leith, Newhaven is a rather dreary-looking fishing village consisting of a few houses on the edge of the sea.[1] The tide was low, laying bare a rocky, blackish beach. Boats had been pulled ashore and lay here and there on their sides. A jetty supported on iron chains rather like a suspension bridge extended a considerable way into the sea. About one mile to the left was Granton Pier, an elegant stone pier used by the ships operating in the Firth of Forth.

'That is where you will embark for Oakley,'[2] Mr B– said. 'The steam packets for London sail from there too.'

'Perfect,' Jacques said. 'Before leaving for Oakley on Monday morning, we can inquire about sailing schedules for London. We may travel south by sea.'

'We'll think it over,' Jonathan said. 'I won't mind if we avoid a sea journey to London.'

At half-past eight the table was laid once again at Mr B–'s and each took a seat. Tea is a solemn ritual in Britain, where it is drunk in huge quantities: more than twelve million kilograms of the plant are imported. The infusing of the beverage is carefully supervised and this important duty devolved upon Miss Amelia who carried it out with charming grace. When the tea had stood for exactly the right number of minutes, she filled her guests' small cups, added a little skimmed milk and crowned the whole with a mist of single cream. Never did Jacques and Jonathan enjoy a better drink, served with such delicacy and kindness. Cakes of a peculiar shape called muffins and specially made for the purpose were served with this unrivalled tea; not even the Emperor of Russia could have drunk a better cup.

Night had fallen. The family and their guests returned to the drawing-room where Jonathan expressed his gratitude for their hospitality by playing and singing delightful melodies, while Jacques consented to accompany him on the organ with a few cleverly improvised basses.[3] Miss Amelia seemed to be very fond of music and she displayed that lively charm and depth of feeling which genuine musicians pour into the interpretation of their own works. She taught Jonathan a few homely tunes from the Highlands which he played on the piano, harmonizing them in a simple yet colourful manner. The melodies, he told Miss Amelia, were somewhat repetitive but of a rich character and texture. They consisted basically in a series of regular intervals and a very simple way of playing Scottish tunes on the piano was to use the black keys only; by chance the design of the piano produced that unexpected result.

To illustrate his words he improvised pretty tunes in this manner, to Miss Amelia's delight. After those sweet compositions, the four Parisian hands rattled out on the piano the bacchanalia of Orpheus which terrified the demure echoes of the house. Then the piano was still, so that it could rest throughout the Sunday and sanctify it with its religious silence. The friends took leave of their charming hosts and agreed to meet Mr B– the following day at one o'clock near the statue of Pitt on George Street.

Notes

[1] MS: edge of the sea. 'It could not compete with the villages on the Normandy coast.'

[2] Oakley. MS: 'Ockley'.

[3] In an interview in 1893, Verne said '[In the 1850s in Paris] my friends were nearly all musicians, and at that period of my life I was a musician myself. I understand harmony, and I think that I may say that, if I had taken to a musical career, I should have had less difficulty than many in succeeding.'

25

Auld Reekie

IT MUST BE ADMITTED that Jacques and Jonathan felt utterly exhausted and their minds had difficulty in absorbing the thousand impressions of that memorable day. Dragging their feet down wide, deserted, poorly-lit streets, they returned to Lambret's Hotel. Fortunately, after such exertions, sleep comes easily.

The following morning they jumped out of bed, dressed rapidly and once again started exploring the city. Their first destination was Calton Hill, to take a closer look at the strange monuments they had noticed from the top of Arthur's Seat.

It was a Scottish Sunday and the streets were bleaker and more deserted than ever, with every single shop puritanically closed. It was a rare passer-by who dared desecrate the desolate paving stones with his

It was a Scottish Sunday and the streets were bleaker and more deserted than ever. (p. 109)

impious feet. All thought and action seemed entombed by the solemn boredom of the Protestant faith, that dry arid wind which blights spirit and heart. Edinburgh Sundays are gloomy indeed.

Calton Hill is not very high and Edinburgh's civic leaders have adorned it with various monuments, all imitations of ancient edifices, in keeping with local taste. Thus, at the bottom of the stone staircase, the Dugald Stewart monument is a copy of the Lantern of Demosthenes;[1] further up, the Observatory is built on the model of the Temple of the Winds, in Athens. At the top of the hill stands the Nelson monument, which is of a great height and topped by a signal for the ships that sail up and down the Forth. This tower has a dismal shape, and is so inelegant it is painful to contemplate.[2] Nearby are the twelve Corinthian columns of the portico of an unfinished building – this is Scotland's National Monument. The project was voted with acclamations in the patriotic surge that followed the battle of Waterloo, in order to commemorate the victory, but funds soon ran dry and a modern, unfinished ruin is all that stands of a building intended to be an exact replica of the Parthenon, that masterpiece of Greek architecture. Up there on Calton Hill, the unfinished portico looks successful, and overall the group of monuments is attractive in that setting, even if, taken individually, each one is poorly designed, nastily cluttered with detail and unstylish. Nonetheless, this architectural attempt to look like something is preferable to looking like nothing, as so many French monuments do.

With its attractive view, Calton Terrace offers the city's fashionable society a place for promenading its boredom – Sundays and holidays excepted, of course, when it is confined indoors. Jacques and Jonathan had the terrace to themselves as they silently gazed out toward the coastline and the North Sea.

'Where shall we lunch?' Jacques asked finally.

'At our usual tavern on the High Street.'

They walked down past the High School,[3] a large Graeco-Egyptian temple that looks as if it has been shipped from Athens with Theseus's compliments, past the prison and along the North Bridge, which overlooks the fruit and vegetable market, to the General Railway Station and the hungrily-desired tavern. No lunch, however: a firmly locked door. They knocked. Nothing. They looked for some other coffee-house – in vain. They inquired where they could find a meal – nowhere! No-one eats on Sundays in Edinburgh or the rest of Scotland. Cooks and tradesmen are at mass or at prayers. Parisians could not be expected to know this and it was on the verge of collapse that they returned to Lambret's Hotel.

'It's a bit too much,' Jacques grumbled. 'You'd think they're all soul and no stomach on Sundays.'

Fortunately, they found plenty to eat and drink at the hotel – too much even, for Jacques fell victim to two pints of Scottish ale he was not sufficiently wary of. He had to rest for an hour and woke up with a bad headache. It was in this condition Jonathan took him to meet Mr B–, near the statue of William Pitt.

The main goal of this new outing was the Castle. They crossed Princes Street Gardens. This ravine, now marvellously landscaped, was once a lake guarding the approach to the citadel. It has been partly filled in with soil brought from the site of the New Town; the lawns are green and refreshing, and everyone is free to stroll over them. Mr B– and his guests rested for a while on a bench in this wonderful garden before crossing Waverley Bridge to reach the high part of town. The bridge spans the second part of the ravine, which is occupied by the General Railway Station, where Edinburgh's various railways converge, including the North British and the Edinburgh and Glasgow. The bridge leads to the Bank of Scotland, a magnificently-situated building, and up to the Lawnmarket, which prolongs the High Street and the Canongate right up to the castle entrance. There, on the Lawnmarket, the clocktower of Victoria Hall raises its Gothic spire. A few yards further on, Mr B– pointed out the house of the poet Allan Ramsay[4] who started as a barber's apprentice before being nicknamed the Scottish Theocritus. He was Scotland's eighteenth-century equivalent of Jasmin, a barber-poet of the Languedoc.[5] The houses on this part of Castle Hill were formerly owned by the Scottish nobility who used them as residences and strongholds. The esplanade in front of the castle is large and has a bronze statue of the Duke of York wearing the apparel of the Order of the Garter.

Edinburgh Castle[6] rises 380 feet above sea level. With his mistaken notion of heights, Jacques found this hard to accept, but he could not argue with their pleasant guide who led them round the inner courtyards, outlining the history of the ancient fort which was known as the Castle of the Maidens, *Castrum Puellarum*, in the time of the minstrel-kings. With Dumbarton, Stirling and Blackness, it formed part of that group of four castles which must be fortified at all times according to the terms of the Union Treaty between the two kingdoms. The Battery is popular with the inhabitants of the old city and it offers a magnificent view over the sea and the surrounding hills. In the Royal Battery, Mr B– pointed out a gigantic 15th-century cannon consisting of iron bars held together by thick hoops. It looks like a gigantic metal cask and it still has a yawning wound in its lacerated side that dates from an explosion on a public holiday.

The visitors were too tired to enter the castle and so they failed to see the Scottish Crown Jewels. From one of the squares, Mr B– showed them the window of that historic chamber where Mary Stuart gave birth to

James VI, who later became James I of England. The poor queen's memory still lives on within those walls and hearts are still moved by the thought of the fairest, best-loved woman of her century.

'And in any case she was half-French,' Jacques said. 'Frenchmen are bound to honour the memory of the Duke of Guise's tragic niece.'

Notes

[1] Did Verne mean the 'Lantern of Diogenes', on the Acropolis?
[2] Robert Louis Stevenson agreed: 'it ranks amongst the vilest of man's handiworks.'
[3] The Royal High School, designated site for the proposed Scottish parliament.
[4] Allan Ramsay (1686–1758) was an exponent of the pastoral tradition in Scottish literature, and lived on Castle Hill. His best-known work is *The Gentle Shepherd.*
[5] Jacques Boé, better-known as Jasmin, was born in Agen in 1798 and he was still living in 1859. This barber-poet who wrote in the old *langue d'Oc* was discovered by Charles Nodier.
[6] MS: 'Mr B– told his guests that' Edinburgh Castle . . .

26

Another pronunciation lesson

'AND NOW, GENTLEMEN,' Mr B– said, 'we shall return to Inverleith Row, where dinner awaits us.'

'Willingly,' Jacques said, 'but do you mind if we take a cab? I'm worn out.'

'No problem. We'll find one at the end of Princes Street, which is downhill all the way.'

A few minutes later, they had crossed the gardens and were being driven in a carriage to Mr B–'s house. Dinner was served with the same hospitality as on the previous evening. The main dish was something called a haggis, a kind of pudding made with meat and barley flour[1] which is peculiar to Scotland, and everyone did great honour to it. After the dessert and its rituals, Miss Amelia set about planning the programme for the visit to the lochs. She had made the same literary and artistic excursion and her excellent memory enabled her to combine times of departure and means of transport to perfection.

The two tourists would journey directly up the Forth to Oakley and from there travel by train to Glasgow via Stirling, returning by way of Loch Lomond and Loch Katrine. Two days would be enough for this splendid outing. Miss Amelia wrote out the itinerary in that fine, elongated hand which is perhaps the only elegant thing the women of Britain have invented. Jacques asked her in English for this precious document, wishing to show off his knowledge. Contorting his jaw, he said:

'*Miss, give me, if you please, one document for reading*' – which he pronounced '*riding*'.

Miss Amelia looked surprised: 'That's pointless, since you'll be going by sea.'

'Pardon me, but I don't see what–'

'Well, you won't be travelling on horseback, will you?'

Jonathan could not help laughing heartily at this exchange.

113

'Jacques has problems with his wonderful pronunciation,' he told Miss Amelia.

'Dear me, what did I ask for?' Jacques asked.

Jonathan explained and it was Miss Amelia's turn to laugh gaily, while poor Jacques, mulling over the subtle difference between *reading* and *riding*, swore to himself he would never let that dreadful language pollute his lips again.

Around ten o'clock the travellers took their leave. They would be seeing the kind family again on their way to Granton Pier the next morning, for a last cup of tea and to leave their portmanteaux, which they did not need for such a short outing.

The weather had been fine until then, but the next morning it looked forbidding. The wind had turned westwards and was herding heavy clouds across the sky.

'Damn!' Jonathan said. 'That looks like rain.'

'It'll give us a different impression of the lochs and mountains,' Jacques said. 'Come on, let's go, instead of complaining.'

They ordered a cab. Jonathan settled their bill at Lambret's Hotel. The rooms were expensive, as indeed all over Britain, and cost the exorbitant sum of five shillings a night. At eight-thirty, they were having morning tea with the B– family.

At nine o'clock the cab left them on the dock beside Granton Pier. The rain started. A strong wind rose and almost carried off Jacques's hat, which was rescued just in time from the precipice by a barefooted young gentleman in tatters. Jacques rewarded him with the gift of one penny, which the lad accepted with cold dignity.

The first thing Jacques did was to inspect the steam packets for London. They were magnificent ships appointed with the quality and comfort that distinguish British shipbuilding. With Jonathan's help, Jacques learned that the passage took at least forty hours, with the most expensive cabins costing twenty shillings. The next sailing was scheduled for the two o'clock tide on the following Wednesday.

'The price seems reasonable, but the journey a bit long and the weather uncertain.' Thus Jonathan, as he studied the powerful breakers beyond the harbour.

'We don't have to decide now,' Jacques said. 'There goes our bell. Come on!'

The *Prince of Wales* was moored alongside the jetty; its funnel was belching out smoke and its boiler rumbled. There was a lot of activity on deck as last-minute travellers rushed up at the sound of the bell. The steamboat calls at the main villages and towns along the Forth and the deck is always crowded with passengers who squat down and do not move until they have arrived.[2] On this journey, they included tradesmen, 'countrymen' and squires. There were also Presbyterian ministers in long black coats and short breeches who stood out in the crowd with their solemnity and fresh complexions. One of them, a singularly handsome young man aged about thirty, stood with his hand resting on his walking-stick in a graceful pose that recalled one of those quaint characters in *The Vicar of Wakefield.*

Despite the rain, which was falling heavily, no passenger sought refuge below deck. Scotsmen, and the British in general, are so used to their unreliable weather they no longer take any notice of it. Furthermore they are experienced travellers and do not load themselves with unnecessary luggage. They wrap themselves in a travelling-rug and revive their spirits with gin or whisky from the flask they always carry – thus, in defiance of rain and wind, warming themselves from within.

The bell rang for the last time and the young Frenchmen went down on to the deck along a steep gangway that made Jonathan dizzy. The chain was hauled ashore and the *Prince of Wales* headed out of the harbour which had sheltered it from the North Sea rollers.

Notes

[1] 'Barley flour' is what Verne wrote, but oatmeal is more usual in a haggis recipe.

[2] Verne returned to this description of the journey on the *Prince of Wales* up the Firth of Forth, with minor changes, in *Les Indes noires* ('The Child of the Cavern'), chapter 2.

27

The Firth of Forth

THE FIRTH OF FORTH, which people in Edinburgh are always talking about, is a long narrow arm of the sea squeezed in between the shores of Fife to the north and the counties of Linlithgow, Edinburgh and Haddington to the south. The Forth, a small river that starts on the slopes of Ben Lomond flows down into the estuary at Kincardine, near Alloa.

The steamer takes three hours to travel from Granton Pier to the innermost tip of the Firth. The strange indentations of the coastline oblige the ship to reach its small ports of call, most of them with landing-stages, by a weaving, circuitous route. Towns, villages and cottages dot the lush, wooded shores – although the French tourists could not see much of this attractive but rain-streaked countryside. They sheltered as best they could under the overhanging bridge-house under the gangway slung between the paddle-boxes, unable to enjoy a comforting smoke since this was allowed only in the bow.

The Firth of Forth is a long narrow arm of the sea squeezed in between the shores of Fife to the north and the counties of Linlithgow, Edinburgh and Haddington to the south. (p. 117)

117

The French tourists could not see much of this attractive but rain-streaked countryside.
(p. 117)

For some time they had been hearing muffled explosions in the western part of the estuary.[1] Jacques tried to work out where they came from, but without success. The explosions grew more distinct once the *Prince of Wales* had passed the village of Aberdour and the island of Inchcolm. Near the large royal burgh of Queensferry, after rounding the fortified isle of Inch Garvie where the Forth is at its narrowest, the steamboat found itself facing a ship of the Royal Navy, a double-decker engaged in firing practice with the guns of its lower battery.

'It's going to hit us!' Jonathan exclaimed.

'That's what it looks like,' Jacques said, 'because you've misjudged its position. Look!'

The ricochet fire produced a weird effect. The cannonball sliced diagonally into the waves before reappearing on the rebound much further on, marking its ducks-and-drakes progress with foaming sprays of water. Jonathan was right to worry, however: a few days later the *Prince of Wales* was hit by a stray cannonball. The British are casual about such things; but fortunately, no-one was hurt.

To starboard they saw Rosyth Castle, formerly home to a branch of the Stuarts from whom Cromwell's mother was descended – a truly singular connection that leaves one pensive 'even in driving rain', Jacques commented, unable to resist the spell of historic associations in such redolent places.

On the left shore, they passed Blackness Castle, which is fortified in keeping with the Union Treaty, then the small harbour of Charlestown,[2] from where Lord Elgin ships the limestone of his huge quarries.[3] The bell announced the landing-stage of Crombie Point.

The weather was at its worst. Lashed by a driving gale, the rain raged in soaking squalls. To make matters worse the steamboat could not reach the landing-stage. So, in the midst of a terrible storm, the young men had to clamber down to a little boat in the middle of the Forth which must be two or three miles wide at this point.

Peering toward the jetty, Jacques thought he could see a lone figure sheltering under a large umbrella.

The *Prince of Wales* steamed on, leaving the little boat adrift in the middle of the Forth. The boatman had to hoist a sail to reach Crombie Point, which he only succeeded in doing after several hopeless attempts. There, they climbed up a ladder fastened to the side of the jetty, its rungs draped in seaweed and wrack left by the outgoing tide. More than once, they almost slipped off and perished, but at last the dripping travellers found themselves shaking clammy hands with the Reverend Mr S–.

'*Soyez les bienvenus, Messieurs,*' he said in his excellent French. 'I do apologize for this unfortunate weather.'

'It takes more than a little rain to worry us,' Jacques said.

'I'm afraid it's getting worse,' the Reverend Mr S— said, 'so I suggest we stop at the inn at the end of the jetty.'

Jacques and Jonathan followed the priest to the isolated inn where his parishioners greeted him warmly. A cheery fire was soon blazing in the hearth and the three travellers disappeared in the heavy steam that rose from their clothes. After a while, the squalls seemed to lessen and they bravely set out for Oakley.

For about a mile, the path wound along a bleak, rocky beach, before turning inland under tall trees from which the rain streamed down. It was impossible to hold a conversation in such conditions and the priest led the way, followed by Jacques, with Jonathan coming last. The path meandered over uneven ground below which lie Scotland's richest coalfields. It was a track intended at best for the little local horses which are akin to the ponies of Northern Scotland. Here and there, an isolated farm was surrounded by tracts of pasture-ground dotted with large herds of cattle that grazed peacefully in the rain. Jacques noticed cows without horns, and tiny sheep with silky wool which looked just like toys. There was no sign of a shepherd for this vast flock – no doubt he was sheltering under some rock – but collies, a local breed renowned for their intelligence and alertness, watched the cows and sheep, rounding up any strays.

The priest pointed out the exceptional fertility of the area they were crossing as they gradually left the Forth behind. In this region of central Scotland's, where dense forests of fir and oak once flourished, wheat, barley and oats are carefully cultivated, producing good harvests, even though the soil is much poorer than in England owing to the damp climate. The countryside was quite unlike that of France. The clumps of trees, the layout of fields with their thick hedges and something in that special atmosphere, created differences the mind could sense rather than figure out. All this awoke in Jacques the emotions produced by a new landscape, the kind of emotions travellers seek far from home. They had been walking for one and a half hours when the priest told them they were approaching Oakley; and indeed they were already in the parkland that surrounds the castle, while the Parisians thought they were still in the open countryside. Beyond a long screen of oaks an elegant sanded drive led them through a renewed squall of rain to a building whose outline they could not see. They entered it through a side door.

Notes

[1] The Firth of Forth is the setting for an incident in *Les Indes noires* ('The Child of the Cavern') too, which centres not on naval manoeuvres but on James Starr's fears of being recognized (chapter 2).

[2] Blackness and Charlestown are in fact on opposite shores.

[3] MS: quarries. 'Culross, with the picturesque ruins of a Cistercian abbey'. Culross is in fact west of Crombie Point.

28

On the traces of Sir Walter Scott

A MANSERVANT, OR SOME KIND of butler dressed in black, received them in a splendid antechamber furnished with beautiful chests and seats.

'Help the gentlemen remove their cloaks and lay out dry clothes for them,' the Reverend Mr S– said and, turning to his guests: 'Shall we warm our spirits with a drink?'

So saying, he preceded them into a spacious dining-room with huge windows and all the refinements of modern luxury. He filled three small glasses with excellent spirits and emptied his own at one go without blinking. Out of politeness Jonathan thought he should imitate him. The powerful drink almost choked him and set him coughing violently.

The priest said: 'You'll now be shown to your rooms where you should find some dry clothes.'

Jacques and Jonathan were led up a regal staircase to elegantly appointed rooms. A special perfume, a dainty attention to furniture and detail suggested these were usually the apartments of a wealthy lady. A spacious bathroom placed in the circular recess of a turret offered all the frivolous accessories indispensable to feminine taste.

The two friends had only to reach out for stockings, slippers and trousers. They realized that the priest had put his own wardrobe at their disposal and they could not help laughing merrily as they slipped into roomy black pants with wide flaps which fastened to the belt.

Thus attired but perfectly comfortable, they went down to the ground floor.

A luxurious drawing-room opened into a study at one end and a conservatory full of rare plants at the other, creating the effect of a long gallery. It is difficult to imagine the amount of light that flows in through those large British windows with projecting bays which offer a view on all sides. This arrangement is common to houses all over the country, since a persistent fog obliges builders to try to capture as much daylight as possible. Being in this gallery was almost like being out of doors; the rain had stopped and a few sunbeams were breaking through the higher clouds.

A fire was blazing in a large, welcoming hearth. An open piano stood before a window. Chairs of all kinds adorned the corners of the drawing-room while in the conservatory there was less mahogany and rosewood and more ornamented china. The drawing-room walls were hung with valuable paintings – exceptional canvases from the Italian school which the priest himself had brought from Rome, and a few Flemish masterpieces. Jacques and Jonathan were amazed to find such luxury in the heart of that untamed countryside.

The castle was resolutely modern and still in its prime. Judged from within, it was obviously built in the Gothic style, which the British have made so popular. The fanciful extravagance of Gothic enables architects to give their imagination a free rein and when they are British one can be sure they will sacrifice everything to comfort, putting a door where it is most convenient, adding a window where it offers the best view, arranging drawing-rooms and bedrooms in the most suitable manner, here raising the ceiling of a hall, there lowering that of a study, placing a cosy nook off a long, high gallery. The overall result is an irregular façade pleasing in its lack of symmetry, since this preference for improvisation over architectural formality creates a certain elegance. There are many small Gothic mansions in Scotland, which are well adapted to local customs and climate.

The meal was in keeping with the aristocratic luxury of the décor. The Reverend Mr S– did the honours with kindly grace; as is customary in Scotland, and out of courtesy for his guests, he invited them to carve the dishes brought before them. Jacques fared rather clumsily with a chicken swimming in a peculiar sauce, but Jonathan coped beautifully with an orange jelly quivering in a bowl of glazed china. Sherry, port and a claret of exceptional vintage flowed plentifully, as did the soda water served in small bottles shaped like baby-bottles which stood in front of the guests' plates. Needless to say, the main course consisted of the inevitable mountain of beef with its inseparable hills of boiled vegetables.

During this Homeric feast, which reminded Jacques of Waverley's banquet with Fergus,[1] the Reverend Mr S– told his guests about the traditions of the region they had crossed and the one they would be visiting.

'You'll be in real Scott territory, gentlemen. You'll see for yourselves how faithfully he captured the spirit of the historic places you'll be visiting and how authentic his descriptions are. For the region is worthy of his boundless genius.'

'Will we meet any Highlanders?' Jonathan asked. 'Have any of the famous clans survived?'

'Certainly,' the Reverend Mr S– replied. 'They no longer have a political role, but some families still command traditional loyalties. The feudal authority of the MacGregors, Douglases, Sutherlands, Macdonalds and Campbells is still recognized. Their followers are their equal before the law, yet they still consider themselves subjects and dependants of their respective chieftains. Each clan is identified by the colour of its tartan.'

'It's a great pity we don't have time to go into all that in more detail,' Jacques said. 'We'll have to be content with a bird's eye view of these traditions, which have survived, as I understand, in the lochs and mountains of Stirlingshire and Argyll.'

'Have no fear, Monsieur Jacques. With a guide like Sir Walter, your journey will be an instructive one. Already he has awakened your feelings to the marvels of the Middle Ages. In Edinburgh you found the old Canongate of his novels and its atmosphere, which he described so well. He won't let you down in the mountains or on the shores of the lochs.'

Jacques questioned the Reverend Mr S– about religious trends in Scotland. He learned that Catholicism was spreading, as in England, despite legal hindrances to its development. With their strong faith, persuasive courtesy and liturgical dignity, Catholic priests were bound to win against the brashness and rigidity of the Protestant ministers. The above comments are even truer of Scotland than of England.

Towards the end of the meal, the butler appeared and informed the priest that a sick person had asked for him. Despite the weather and the distance involved, Mr S– took leave of his guests immediately, entrusting them to the care of the bailie, who would show them around the park. After one last handshake, he disappeared. He would not be seeing his guests again.

'Self-denial and devotion, that's their motto,' Jacques told his friend as they left the table.

Note

1 *During this Homeric feast (. . .) with Fergus*: this phrase was added by Verne in the margin. It is later echoed in *Le Rayon vert* ('The Green Ray'), chapter 14. [This is of course a reference to *Waverley*, chapter 20.]

29

By train to Glasgow

ITH HIS BREECHES of striped velvet, his leather gaiters and Scottish bonnet, the bailie of Oakley was a fine-looking fellow. All he needed was a dirk in his belt and a plaid over his shoulder. He looked as if he were descended from one of those loyal tenant farmers who used to devote themselves body and soul to their masters. He placed himself at the visitors' disposal and although Jonathan found his mixture of Gaelic and Anglo-Saxon difficult to understand, he worked out that the good man's son had fought in the Crimean War alongside the French.[1] He seemed to be very proud of this. Guided by him, they completed their tour of the castle, not missing a single detail. They had to see everything, including the quiet, austere

The stacks of a coalpit smoked peacefully. (p. 126)

library and a natural history display which was guarded by a huge stuffed tiger. Jonathan, who was the first to enter the room, did not expect to come nose to nose with any such beast, and he let out a cry of fright which set the Scotsman laughing as probably no one has ever laughed in Scotland.

On a rooftop platform they discovered, swathed in leather, a telescope that swivelled on a central pivot and could be trained on every inch of the horizon. From up there the view spread out over a huge expanse which ranged from bleak wild heaths to tilled fields. Behind the castle, about two miles away, the stacks of a coalpit smoked peacefully. This mine belonged to Mr S– and its substantial output of coal provided him with gas to light not only the castle but the drive and walks in the park which were lined with elegant lanterns on pilasters. In England and Scotland even small villages and farms are lit thanks to this distillation of coal, since all you need do in this generous land is dig a hole for perennial heat and light to gush forth.

The façade of the castle, before which stretched a large lawn, produced a charming impression with its quaint asymmetry, its irregular roofs, its Gothic gables and turrets. The upkeep of this façade was so meticulous the building looked like a brand-new dolls' house that had just come out of its box; and one felt that the whim which had placed it there one bright day could just as easily move it elsewhere to please its owner.

'Jonathan, wouldn't you like to live in a jewel like this and in such a beautiful area?' Jacques said. 'Work would surely be pleasant, life sweet, and happiness easy!'

'What a brave remark, from a dedicated Parisian who hates the countryside.'

'I hate the countryside around Paris. In the end it's always the city, only with fewer and fewer trees since they are cut down to make room for avenues. But look at that scenery and those thick copses, smell that breeze scented with wild heather, which blows down deep glens; hear its plaintive melody in the Strathdearie pipes[2] – to echo Scott – and tell me what remote resemblance all this bears to the scrubbed, shaven and shorn countryside around Paris, where there are no wild scents and the consumptive air lacks the strength to produce real winds. Some day, if I can afford it, I'll buy a sweet cottage in this area and live here like a real Highlander.'

'Idle dreams,' Jonathan said. 'You'll have to seek your cottage elsewhere. Foreigners aren't allowed to own even a square inch of these islands.'

'What a shame!'

After walking round the castle and along the wide, sanded avenues of the park, they were led by the bailie to the greenhouses adjoining the *lodges* where the horses were stabled. The layout and exposure were so perfect the greenhouses contained the most beautiful ripe fruit in the world. The vine was already sagging under the weight of outsize grapes. It was a natural laboratory where all kinds of early fruit and vegetables could be grown to satisfy the palates of the castle occupants.

On leaving this crystal palace, the guard offered to take the visitors to the coal mines,[3] but it was getting late, so they returned to the castle. Jacques and Jonathan removed Mr S–'s clothes with merry gratitude and slipped into their own again, which were now dry. The bailie took them into the dining room for a stirrup cup of whisky, the *doch an dorroch*, in accordance with Scottish etiquette, which they accepted. He then drove them to Oakley station to catch the train from Dunfermline, which would take them to Glasgow via Stirling. There they thanked their pleasant guide with a generosity that was more French than British and took leave of the hospitable S– estate at the railway station.

Soon afterwards they reached Stirling, where they had to change trains. They saw nothing at all of the town. To reach the departure platform, they had to cross the station over a kind of covered bridge below which engines roared. Jonathan bought tickets for Glasgow, which cost him three shillings and threepence for a second-class fare. The railway attendants were so unpleasant and in such short supply he found it very difficult to decide which was the right train. Finally, with Jacques following, he climbed into a compartment already crowded with elderly women. They seemed to resent this male company and when Jonathan happened to say he was going to Glasgow they eagerly pointed out that it was the wrong train. They were right: the train would have taken the two tourists back to Oakley. The engine of the Glasgow train whistled as they climbed down hastily and dashed into a compartment with French impetuosity.

After Stirling the railway moved away from the Forth. At this point the river separates the Lowlands from the hills, hence the local saying that the 'Forth is the bridle of the Highlanders'. In *Rob Roy*, Walter Scott claims that the river is more English than Scottish in character, but Jacques could not check the truth of this. The train was taking him southwards again and without admitting it he was displeased since his yearnings drew him continually northwards. He cheered up, however, when Jonathan told him that their visit to the lochs would take them into higher latitudes.

A few miles from Stirling, the railway line passes near the village of Bannockburn where Robert the Bruce won a terrible victory over the English king, Edward II. The line then follows the Forth and Clyde canal, which a great number of flatboats use, their masts mingling indistinctly with the trees. Evening was falling when Castlecary appeared, with the

127

Finally the train plunged into a long tunnel and reached the centre of Glasgow. (p. 128)

remains of the Roman wall Agricola built to hold back the independent Caledonians of the north.[1] The conquerors of the world were stopped by that brave, proud nation that still suffers under English domination. Finally the train plunged into a long tunnel and reached the centre of Glasgow.

Notes

[1] In 1856, Paul, Jules Verne's brother, took part in the Crimean War as an officer aboard a troopship, the *Cassini*.

[2] *the Strathdearie pipes*: Verne uses the phrase again in *Le Rayon vert* ('The Green Ray'), chapter 2.

[3] MS: coal mines. 'Jacques would have liked to visit them' but . . . The frustration expressed in that short sentence will generate *Les Indes noires* ('The Child of the Cavern'), set in a Scottish mine.

[4] The Antonine wall.

30

Cheshire cheese and Northern Lights

THE MOMENT THEY STEPPED out of the station, the two travellers found themselves on an attractive square with a small enclosed garden where they could vaguely make out a few columns adorned with statues. It was too dark to see anything clearly – even the name, George Square, which they read with some difficulty. Noticing Comrie's Royal Hotel, they entered and were received by some charming young women with winning manners. Treading on his friend's linguistic toes, Jacques mumbled a few words that tried hard to be English. The young misses proved very obliging and, gathering that he had asked for a room with two beds, arranged for the Frenchmen to be shown up to the first floor.

After a good wash the guests went down to the dining-room and sat at a big table after asking for supper. While the meal was being prepared, Jacques studied a few prints of Edinburgh which hung on the walls. He was delighted to see those familiar streets again and thought proudly: 'I've been there!'

As he moved along, examining the prints, his nose was bothered by a strange, not to say sickening, smell.

'What can that be?' he asked Jonathan.

'I've no idea, but whatever it is, it's horrible. It's like being on a steamer when the sea's rough and you feel seasick.' He knew what he was talking about. Suddenly in a corner of the room, he pointed to a dresser.

'There's the culprit!'

'What is it?'

'A huge Cheshire cheese someone forgot.'

'You mean, it's forgotten itself,' Jacques said.

When the waiter arrived they persuaded him, with some difficulty, to remove the offending viand.

After a suitable fare of cold mutton, York ham and tea, the two friends took to the streets. They wished to get a feel of the city by night. Fine

129

Chance led them to the edge of the Clyde and to Glasgow Bridge. (p. 131)

squares, wide streets, black houses, dark as shops and depressing as factories, some vague resemblance to Liverpool, the unpoetic details of an industrial city: these were the glimpses they had.

'This is no longer Scotland,' Jacques said. 'I expect we'll wake up to the sound of hammering in an atmosphere of industrial fumes.'

Chance, that god beloved of travellers, led them to the edge of the Clyde and to Glasgow Bridge. Several cargo ships and steamers were anchored near the bridge, which is the last link between the two banks of the Clyde before the North Channel. As they stood there they noticed a large red glow. Flashes of lightning and bright trails seemed to cross a big expanse of sky which looked like a burning vault. Jonathan decided it was a fire, Jacques thought it must be the glow from a blast furnace. They were both wrong and later understood that they had unknowingly seen the famous aurora borealis of 30 August, 1859.

They returned to Comrie's Royal Hotel down wide streets lined with houses. Jacques read the names, Argyle Street and Buchanan Street. Their day of rain, sun and wind had been a tiring one and they wanted to be up early the next morning to get a better idea of the city before setting out for the lochs.

Wide beds with narrow sheets that made them seem all the wider awaited them in a huge room with painted beams. The atmosphere was somewhat funereal and Jonathan could not help comparing his friend and himself to the young Princes in the Tower, the sons of King Edward IV. Remembering the painting by Paul Delaroche,[1] he shuddered at the memory of the ruthless Tyrrel. Still, since they were not of sufficiently royal pedigree to be murdered in their sleep and having no Richard III in their family, they awoke with the dawn: simple, eager visitors. After settling the bill, they hurried out of the hotel.

Jonathan was amazed to find the streets thronged with busy crowds – until Jacques informed him that the city had grown from 75 000 to 350 000 inhabitants. In Glasgow they rediscovered Liverpool, complete with public buildings blackened by soot and fog. In the middle of George Square stood monuments to Scott and James Watt, two men brought together in one remembrance. But for the inscriptions, the statues looked so very much alike that the novelist might have been mistaken for the inventor of the steam engine and the engineer for the creator of *The Fair Maid of Perth*.

The day had begun inauspiciously, with that drizzle peculiar to the British Isles which is not so much wet as dirty. Nevertheless the Frenchmen were there for sightseeing so despite the rain they walked down George Street to Glasgow Cathedral, which is of some fame.

'Always the same names and the same streets,' Jacques said.

At this early hour countrymen from outside the city were driving to the city markets, their horses harnessed to carts laden with fruit and vegetables. '*Whig a more! Whig a more!* Faster!' they called to the horses, using the phrase which has become the watchword of the liberal party. As for the Tories, who are royalists, they owe their name to '*tory me*', 'give me', which corresponds to the phrase 'Your money or your life' used by French highwaymen.[2]

When the black stream of an open drain barred the way of the countrymen, they just removed their shoes and carried them as they waded across the muddy slime.

'Shoes are certainly useless for wading across a stream,' Jonathan said, 'but somehow I don't think I'll remove mine.'

Glasgow Cathedral is dedicated to St Mungo. It displays different stages of Gothic architecture and has a high, massive steeple. It is the only religious monument in Scotland to have been spared by the fanatical Reformers and is worth seeing on that account. To his regret, Jacques was unable to enter the cathedral. The door was closed and remained firmly so despite his knocking – Protestantism obviously does not practise 'knock and it shall be opened'. He had to be content with the memory of Scott's vivid descriptions and a visit to the necropolis on the neighbouring hill. It was here that Osbaldistone and Andrew Fairservice made their way on reaching Glasgow where Rob Roy was in hiding. This then was the melancholy cemetery with the tombstones where Scott thought he could read the prophet's words: 'Lamentations and mourning and woe!'

Notes

[1] *Paul Delaroche.* (1797–1856). This 'academic' painter sought inspiration in English history. Thus his *Cromwell before the coffin of Charles I*, which was exhibited in the *Salon* of 1831. In 1859 the Musée des Beaux-Arts of Nantes had in its possession *l'Enfance de Pic de la Mirandole*, which was painted in 1842. *Les Enfants d'Edouard* date from 1831 and are inspired by Shakespeare's *Richard III* (Act IV, 2,3). Verne may have seen the painting in the Louvre.

[2] *Whig a more* and *tory me* sic in Verne's original text. Whiggamore originally applied to Scottish insurgents. Verne seems to think that 'tory' means 'give'; according to the OED, 'tory' is the 'Anglicized spelling of the Irish *tóraidhe*, pursuer, *tóir*, to pursue'. In *Cinq semaines en ballon* ('Five Weeks in a Balloon') Joe the Scot uses the phrase 'whig a more' to encourage the elephant towing the *Victoria* (chapter 17). Verne drew these phrases directly from Scott.

31

Of sausages and umbrellas

A FTER VISITING THAT DREARY and solitary place, the tourists hunted for a cab, since there was still a lot to see and not much time. A large carriage lined with Utrecht velvet offered them welcome shelter from the rain. Jonathan asked the coachman to drive them to the harbour then down the city's main streets and into its parks. The cab horse trotted off towards Glasgow Bridge.

The streets in the business and shopping quarters are handsome. They are lined with countless banks, halls, museums, workhouses, institutions, municipal buildings, hospitals, assembly rooms and clubhouses. Glasgow also has an athenaeum and a stock exchange. All these buildings are heavily addicted to cumbersome, often inelegant columns. The British craze for columns is surely greater than their passion for horses – although they sometimes perch bronze casts of the latter on stone examples of the former, a combination that does not enhance a building. The harbour was bustling with activity. Gigantic wharves stretched out along the quaysides of the Clyde, bulging with millions of pounds' worth of freight. After Liverpool harbour, however, Glasgow's was not really interesting so the cab drove past briskly.

From there, where did the shrewd cabby go? To which districts did he take his clients? Into which suburbs? They never found out. All they remembered was following the wide circular drive of a hilly park overlooked by layer upon layer of grand, recently-built houses. Later, when Jacques studied a plan of Glasgow, he could not find his park, which he decided belonged to the marvellous dreamland where fancy roves during the fair nights of childhood.

Wherever it was, in due course the cabby returned them to George Square. Jonathan overtipped him and they set off in search of a coffee-room for lunch. They found one in Gordon Street, near the Exchange. There was nothing special about the meal, except that they were served cold salmon with vinegar but not a drop of oil. After this meal they

133

passed the time until their departure strolling up and down the streets around the station, with Jacques interpreting signs as usual and making unexpected comments.

'Don't you find the British have magnificent names?' he asked. 'I find them superior to our French names, with those rich, resonant syllables which look as good as they sound.'

'That's because you're unfamiliar with the language,' Jonathan said. 'I doubt the locals are as impressed as you are. How would you like being called Taylor, Bacon, or Fox?'

'I'd love it. They sound so distinguished.'

'Yet what would you say if you were called *Tailleur, Lard* or *Renard*? I expect any common French name would be highly sought after in Britain, just as a Mr Horsebum would sound very *chic* in France. Don't you see? It's the same in all languages: Aquado in Spanish, Buoncompagni in Italian, Zimmermann, Schneider or Schumacher in German. Why, even Mr Rothschild, whose real name is Mayer anyway, is but a baron with a red shield to people who speak German.'

'What can I say? Your polyglot brilliance leaves me speechless,' Jacques said.

Conversing in this way, they passed a pork butcher's shop where they saw an unusual steam-operated machine. It was very ingenious: a live pig was placed at one end and it came out at the other in the form of appetizing sausages.

A train would take them through Dumbarton and Balloch to the southern shore of Loch Lomond. (p. 135)

'What a people!' Jacques exclaimed. 'What genius to apply steam to *charcuterie*! No wonder the British are the masters of the world! One day they'll design a 500 horsepower machine to convert the natives of Oceania. You just wait and see!'

'It couldn't be worse than their missionaries,' Jonathan said.

'After such a discovery,' Jacques said, 'it's time to leave Glasgow.'

They made for the station of the Edinburgh and Glasgow Railway to catch a train which would take them through Dumbarton and Balloch to the southern shore of Loch Lomond. For eleven pence, Jonathan bought third-class seats and they entered a compartment where hardened cattle would have felt ill at ease. There were no doors, let alone glass in the windows, and when the rain began falling more heavily the travellers had to shelter under half-open umbrellas.

Jonathan said: 'The British are so unaccustomed to the sun they use umbrellas to provide shade – which is why they call them umbrellas.'

32

On board the *Prince Albert*[1]

THE JOURNEY WAS SHORT, fortunately; there are barely twenty miles between Glasgow and Balloch. The train passed through Dumbarton, a Royal Burgh and county capital strikingly perched at the estuaries of the Clyde and Leven. Its castle, still fortified in keeping with the terms of the Union treaty, perches on the twin peaks of a basalt crag. Mary Stuart sailed from Dumbarton to become the Queen of France. Later, the castle was once more associated with French history when the British government contemplated holding Napoleon there after 1815.[2] Dumbarton instead of St Helena: in either case a rock, expressive of British hatred for the enemy who had trusted to their honour.

Soon the train stopped in Balloch, not far from a wooden jetty which led down to Loch Lomond.

'Ah! My very first loch!' Jacques exclaimed.

'And your first *real* mountain!' Jonathan added. 'The ones you've seen so far were only make-believe mountains, pocket-sized ones for Parisian eyes.'

They dashed out of the station and down on to the jetty, where they boarded a steamer, the *Prince Albert*; they bought two passages to Inversnaid on the far side of the lake, paying two shillings and sixpence each.

'That's expensive for a thirty-mile crossing. But what a crossing! Do you realize, Jonathan? We're in MacGregor country!'

The first, overwhelming impression of Loch Lomond is of countless delightful islands of every shape and size imaginable. The *Prince Albert* weaved its way between them, skirting their rugged outlines and revealing a myriad different countrysides: here a fertile plain, there a solitary glen, elsewhere a forbidding ravine bristling with age-old rocks. Ancient legends clung to every shore, and the history of this land is written in these gigantic characters of islands and mountains. The loch,

The Prince Albert *set its course for Ben Lomond. (p. 139)*

which is about four or five miles wide at this point, brought to Jacques's mind the vivid descriptions Walter Scott's rival,[3] Fenimore Cooper, wrote of Lake Ontario and its thousand isles, for nature seemed here to have used every trick to vary the scenery. A rocky island bearing no trace of vegetation rears up its jagged crags beside the green rounded rumps of a neighbour; the larch and birch of another protest, with their verdant boughs, at the yellow, dried-up heather of the next; and yet all bathe in the serene equality of the lake's waters. Near Balmaha, which marks the gateway to the Highlands, Jacques noticed a few scattered tombstones: it was the burial-ground of the old Clan MacGregor.

Although the loch was still wide, its shores appeared to close in gradually as the boat drew towards the small harbour of Luss. Despite the

The first impression of Loch Lomond is of countless delightful islands. (p. 137)

driving rain, the two friends remained intrepidly on deck, unwilling to lose a single detail of the varied scenery. As Jacques watched the mist for a glimpse of Ben Lomond, he felt himself steeped in a wild and powerful poetry, recognizing in those sheer cliffs and dark, smooth waters the emotions he had first discovered in his favourite novels. It seemed to him as if Scotland's legendary heroes were born again in this captivating Highland realm.

After calling at Luss, the *Prince Albert* set its course for Ben Lomond, on the opposite shore. The mountain appeared at last, its feet lapped by the waters of the loch, its head hidden in the clouds. At first Jacques found it difficult to accept that it was over a thousand metres high: he expected other sensations from such heights and needed time to adjust to such a grand perspective. Soon, however, the peak emerged from the clouds and the mountain stood revealed in all its majesty – 'Stern, wild majesty!' exclaimed Jacques as he grabbed his friend's arm. 'Look at that! You must be able to see half of Scotland from up there'.

'We'll always regret we never had time to climb to the top of Ben Lomond,' Jonathan said.

'To think the whole mountain belongs to the Duke of Montrose. Can you imagine! His Grace owns a mountain the way a citizen of Paris has a bowling-green in his garden. Look, Jonathan! Look!'

The steamer was approaching Ben Lomond and the loch was shrinking rapidly. This Ben is the last in the Grampian Mountains,

Ben Lomond appeared at its most impressive; from its green base to its bare peak. (p. 140)

which are separated by long solitary glens. *Ben, glen, den* – all these words are of Celtic origin. The clan of the MacGregors had its seat in the clachans, the stone villages on the western shore of the lake, at the very base of the mountain which is illuminated on clear nights by the pale rays of the moon, locally called MacFarlane's lantern.[4] The whole area bears witness to the Macgregors' heroic deeds. Nearby, cruel skirmishes stained desolate gorges with Jacobite and Hanoverian blood; harsh echoes still ring out Rob Roy's several names: MacGregor Campbell!

At the village of Tarbet, on the far shore, the steamer deposited travellers bound for Inveraray. From that part of the lake, Ben Lomond appeared at its most impressive; from its green base to its bare peak, its gigantic flanks were striped with torrents which seemed from afar to shimmer like liquid plates of silver. The way those vertiginous waterfalls sprang from invisible faults to crash into unknown chasms was startling and fantastical.

As the steamer skirted the mountain, the scenery grew steadily more precipitous, the shores barren and rocky, with just a few lonely trees here and there, a willow perhaps, whose branches provided hangmen with nooses more economical than flax.

'Walter Scott considered Loch Lomond the fairest of lochs and Ben Lomond the monarch of mountains,' Jacques said, 'and I fully share his patriotic enthusiasm.'

The scenery grew steadily more precipitous, the shores barren and rocky. (p. 140)

Notes

[1] With some variations, Verne drew on chapters 32 and 33 for his descriptions in *Les Indes noires* ('The Child of the Cavern'), chapter 18. The *Prince Albert* became the *Sinclair*, a surname Verne used in chapter 16 of this book.

[2] The facts concerning Napoleon's captivity are mentioned by Nodier in *Promenade de Dieppe aux montagnes d'Ecosse* (see note to chapter 1).

[3] Fenimore Cooper is one of the authors Verne refers to frequently.

[4] *which is illuminated (. . .) MacFarlane's lantern* was added by Verne in the margin. It is mentioned in *Waverley*: 'The Clan of Mac-Farlane, occupying the fastnesses of the western side of Loch Lomond, were great depredators on the Low Country, and as their excursions were made usually by night, the moon was proverbially called their lantern' (Scott, Note 1 to chapter 9 of vol II, 1895 edition).

33

On the roof of a coach

INVERSNAID CAME INTO VIEW and the two friends disembarked. Near the landing-stage, a rain-swollen torrent hurtled into the lake from a fair height, as if placed there by some enterprising businessman for the enjoyment of tourists. A light, swaying bridge danced over the foaming waters and Jacques dragged Jonathan onto it for a closer view of the raging fall. In a few minutes they were opposite the rocky gash from which a cloud of liquid dust swirled out, and below their feet they heard and felt the roar of liquid frenzy. From the bridge they overlooked the whole lake, where the *Prince Albert* was like a dot in space.

Time, however, was short; the coaches that travel between Loch Lomond and Loch Katrine were waiting, their horses already harnessed. The travellers hurried to Inversnaid hotel where, less from thirst than a yearning for local colour, Jacques asked for a glass of usquebaugh.[1] Out here in the Highlands he found the word colourful, but the drink did not come up to the expectations of its Gaelic name. It was simply whisky with a bitter flavour and he pulled a wry face as he praised the merits of this Highland drink.

The carriages had been newly replaced by the Earl of Breadalbane, whose ancestors formerly provided the outlawed Rob Roy with wood and water,[2] and they displayed the pomp, class and comfort that one associates with British coaches. The doors were stamped with the Breadalbane crest, but despite the driving rain, no-one chose to sit inside. Instead, all the travellers climbed onto the roof where they settled down, determined not to miss a single detail. Oblivious of wind and rain, women wrapped in long shawls of threadbare tartan cashmere climbed up the ladder. Dressed in a livery faced with red, the coachman gathered up the reins of his four splendid horses and the carriage moved up the mountainside, following the twisting torrent.

The road was steep and as it climbed the shape of the mountains seemed to change. Ahead, on the far shore of the lochs, Jacques[3] could see a long line of peaks, with the Arrochar Hills overlooking the glen of Inveruglas. Ben Lomond rose to the left, revealing its precipitous northern flank. It was a strange landscape, stamped with the stern romance of old Caledonia. This bleak, mountainous area situated between Loch Lomond and Loch Katrine was formerly known as Rob Roy's country. The valley they were ascending was linked by a narrow pass to the glen of Aberfoyle where, on the edge of a small lake, Loch Ard, the tragic incidents described in *Rob Roy* took place. The base of the range is formed of sinister-looking limestone rocks mixed with boulders which time and the elements have hardened like cement. Huddled among ruined sheep folds, miserable hovels like animal dens called *brochs* left one wondering whether they sheltered human beings or wild beasts. A few children with hair bleached by the weather watched the carriages go by in wide-eyed wonder. Jacques pointed all these things out to Jonathan, telling him the story of these mysterious glens. It was here that the worthy Bailie Nicol Jarvie, loyal son of his father the deacon, was detained by the Lennox militia on the orders of the Duke of Montrose: this was where he remained suspended by the seat of his pants, which were fortunately cut from good Scottish cloth, not from 'rotten French camlet'.[1] Close to where the Forth

'Those are cairns,' Jacques said. 'In former times anyone who went by added a stone to honour the memory of the hero buried underneath them.' (p. 145)

springs from Ben Lomond, one can still see the ford where Rob Roy escaped from the Duke of Montrose's troopers. One cannot take a step in this exceptional region without coming across events which inspired Walter Scott's rousing echoes of the Clan MacGregor's call to arms.

After scaling the bank of the torrent, the carriage reached a lesser glen with neither trees nor water. It was blanketed with mean coarse heather, and here and there stones were piled in the shape of pyramids.

'Those are cairns,' Jacques said. 'In former times anyone who went by added a stone to honour the memory of the hero buried underneath them. Hence the belief that it's bad luck to pass a cairn without offering a stone to pay last respects. If that tradition had survived to this day, those heaps would now be hills! What a country! Broken ground lends itself to poetry, I'm sure. In all lands, mountains stimulate the imagination. If the Greeks had lived in a country as flat as our French Landes or Beauce, they would never have invented mythology.'

Soon the road wound down the gorge of a narrow glen where one expected to come across mischievous goblins like Meg Merrilies's Scottish brownies. The other tourists gazed around in cold indifference, with no trace of enthusiasm, wonder or indeed any other emotion, as if they considered the excursion a chore, just another part of their tour of Scotland.

'What a pity we're not alone,' Jacques thought. 'You need solitude to respond to the poetry of these valleys and mountains.'

Leaving the small Loch Arklet[5] on the right, the carriage climbed a steep winding slope to reach the inn of Stronachlachar on the edge of Loch Katrine. It had taken the *Prince Albert* two and a half hours for the thirty-mile crossing of Loch Lomond and the carriage one hour for the five miles from Inversnaid to Loch Katrine. After handing the Earl of Breadalbane's coachman the tip he demanded imperiously, the two friends climbed down.

Notes

[1] *usquebaugh* is also drunk by the Melville brothers in *Le Rayon vert*, ('The Green Ray'), chapter 14.

[2] *wood and water*: the shelter of their woods and lakes.

[3] MS: Jacques 'who was travelling backwards' could see ... Once again, Verne had his characters travelling backwards, in keeping with the title of the book.

[4] *Bailie Nicol Jarvie* is a character in *Rob Roy*. [The phrase 'rotten French camlet' is Scott's, from the same novel (chapter 31). Originally a costly eastern fabric, possibly made of camel's hair, but now chiefly of wool and goat's hair, 'camlet' is used here in a meaning akin to the French 'camelote', shoddy goods.

[5] The name 'Artelet', as Verne seems to have written for Arklet, may have inspired the surname T Artelett, a teacher in *L'Ecole des Robinsons*. Verne frequently turned to geography to find names for his characters, including Captains Hatteras and Antifer.

34

From Loch Katrine to Stirling

A FEW METRES FROM the inn, a small ferry bobbed up and down on the water. It was called the *Rob Roy*, of course.

The passengers from the *Prince Albert* were joined by travellers from Aberfoyle, two of whom carried knapsacks and stout sticks which suggested they had been walking in the mountains. Jacques gazed at

*Loch Katrine is only ten miles long and at first its banks
are wild and sparsely wooded. (p. 148)*

The rustic musician played a sweet, gentle melody. (p. 148)

them enviously as the single-screw steamer chugged off. The motor had no condenser and the ferry released a puff of steam with each piston stroke, just like a railway engine.

Loch Katrine is only ten miles long and at first its banks are wild and sparsely wooded, although the range of nearby hills is imbued with poetic charm. The main scenes of Scott's *Lady of the Lake* take place on the shores of this placid loch and the airy form of the beautiful Helen Douglas still seems to glide over the water.

Jacques was daydreaming happily when the sound of a pibroch brought him back to reality. A Scotsman in Highland garb was warming up his bagpipes in the stern.[1]

'Take care,' Jonathan warned. 'He's going to play us the *Trovatore*.'

'That would be a crime,' Jacques said.

This time, however, the Parisians were spared the musical craze of the day. The rustic musician played a sweet, gentle melody, one of those simple pieces which express a national mood and seem to have been composed by no-one, as if they were the natural song of sighing winds, murmuring waters and whispering leaves. Jonathan moved nearer the Scotsman to take down the music which he wrote out in his notebook as a series of numbers:

$$\frac{2}{4} - \dot{1}\,\overline{7\,6}\,|\,\overline{5\,\dot{6}\,\dot{7}}\,\dot{1}\,|\,\overline{3\,3\,5}\,\overline{4\,3}\,|\,\overline{1\,1\,5\,5}\,|\,\dot{1}\,\overline{7\,6}\,|\,\overline{5\,\dot{6}\,\dot{7}}\,\dot{1}$$

$$\overline{3\,3\,5\,4\,3}\,|\,1\,.\,\overline{5\,4}\,|\,\overline{5\,1\,5\,5}\,|\,\overline{1\,7\,6}\,\overline{7\,1}\,.\,|\,\overline{7\,5\,6}\,\widehat{6}\,x\,4$$

$$\overline{5\,5\,6\,7}\,|\,\dot{1}\,\overline{7\,6}\,|\,\overline{5\,\dot{6}\,\dot{7}}\,\dot{1}\,|\,\overline{3\,3\,5\,4\,3}\,7\,.\,.$$

Having done so, he took a closer look at the instrument. He noted that Scottish bagpipes have three drones of different sizes, the biggest being in G, with the second and third drones one octave higher than the biggest (bass) one. The chanter has eight holes, which gives a scale in G major, with a natural F. The French musician made a note of these combinations with the intention of using them some day.

The western shore of Loch Katrine is greener, gentler, more civilized than the opposite one and it is squeezed between two high mountains, Ben An and Ben Venue. Shaded paths wind along the lake before disappearing into close thickets. Altogether, the area presented a novel aspect to the two Frenchmen, who had reached the northernmost point of their journey.

The western shore of Loch Katrine is greener, gentler, more civilized. (p. 149)

The *Rob Roy* left them in a cool, secluded vale with moss-carpeted roads and cheery, fertile land. The carriages for Callander were already waiting and the young men hurried to find seats. They perched up on top near the coachman and Jacques turned one last time to bid goodbye to those magnificent landscapes whose sublime beauty defies the imagination.

Weatherbeaten and exhausted, Jacques led Jonathan to a kind of alehouse. (p. 151)

Eight or nine miles separate Loch Katrine from Callander. The ground is rough and hilly, and carriages cover most of the distance at a walking pace. A mile and a half along the road is the Trossachs Hotel, a gloomy-looking new mansion. With their exogenous crinolines spread out around them, female visitors sat on the terrace contemplating Loch Achray, a miniature lake in a bowl of delightful symmetry.

During the journey the coachman acted as guide, showing off his erudition as in a loud voice he named the ruins, glens, mountains and local clans. His speech was too Scottish for Jonathan to grasp more than fragments of his instructive narrative. Even so he gathered that Glen Finglas runs northwards and that the shores of Loch Venachar are covered with dismal copsewood. These and many more details were well worth the tip the canny coachman demanded when the coach reached Callander's long street, after driving through changing landscapes and over a stone bridge which spanned a torrent where dark waters foamed over black rocks.

Weatherbeaten and exhausted, Jacques led Jonathan to a kind of alehouse for a pint of that common yet excellent ale known as twopenny.

A newly-built railway line linked Callander to Stirling. From there the men could travel on to Edinburgh, but they decided to stop overnight so as to visit the town the next morning. They got into a second-class compartment, reaching Stirling station an hour later.

Finding a meal was their first preoccupation, which was understandable, considering they had left Glasgow on a light lunch, crossed the lochs and travelled until eight in the evening without eating anything. They looked for an hotel and found the Golden Lion, which seemed to be suitable. Soon afterwards they were sitting with strangers at a table loaded with the familiar ham, beef and tea.

Jacques watched one of the respectable British guests call for a boiled egg after his dessert and swallow it whole. He could not resist doing the same and he has maintained ever since that a fresh egg is the only way to round off a meal.

After their meal a giggling girl led the travellers to adjoining rooms on the top floor where weariness and digestion soon rocked them asleep under canopies hung with long curtains of white cotton.

Note

1 *bagpipes*: Verne wrote 'piper bag', which he also used wrongly in *Les Enfants du Capitaine Grant* (Captain Grant's Children), Part I, chapter 5, meaning 'bagpiper'.

35

What a Highlander looks like

THE SUN REAPPEARED the next morning and when it entered their rooms they found it impossible to resist the invitation of its gracious rays. First, they discussed their journey from Edinburgh to London. It seemed impossible to arrive in the Scottish capital before the steam-ship sailed from Granton. Besides, the sea voyage would take up too much time, whereas they could travel by train overnight, leaving Edinburgh at eight in the evening. They therefore settled for this speedier form of transport.

The Royal Burgh of Stirling is built on uneven ground at the mouth of the Forth. From their hotel, the Golden Lion, a street led up a kind of hill covered with monuments which puzzled Jacques; the place might have been a cemetery or a pleasure ground, there being little difference between the two in Scotland. From this mound, they could see the battlements of Stirling Castle, where Mary Stuart's coronation took place. Cromwell and General Monk besieged the proud-looking fort, a defiant pile firmly planted on its haunches, like a stolid trooper. A steep slope led up to the postern, where Highlanders in dress uniform stood on guard.

Except for the leather shield or 'targe', with its steel pike, the Highland guards' uniform is a copy of the old national costume. On their heads they wear the Scottish bonnet, with a plume stuck in a steel badge. Below the scarlet shortcoat fall the countless pleats of the kilt, a kind of petticoat cut from green chequered cloth which reaches to the knees. The thighs are bare, hence the proverb 'ye canna take the breeks aff a Hieland-man'. The hose worn below the knees are criss-crossed with garters which Rob Roy could tie with his long arms without stooping. A tartan cloak or plaid is draped from the belt to the shoulder, where it is fastened with a metal brooch or clasp. To round off the costume, the *philabeg*, a kind of goatskin pouch decorated with tassels, hangs from the belt on the front of the kilt. The purse of this *philabeg*, which is enough to hold a Scotsman's whole fortune, is called a *sporran*, as Jonathan learned from one of the castle sentries; the dagger, or *dirk*, is stuck in the belt and the officers of these splendid regiments carry the long claymores or longswords their ancestors used to wield.[1]

From the castle esplanade the view stretches over the Scottish Lowlands. To the north-west, Jacques caught a last glimpse of Ben Lomond and Ben Ledi who raised their heads over the brow of the distant horizon. The day had deigned to rise cloudless, and the peaks were distinct despite the light morning mist. To the west, at the entrance of the town, the Forth flowed under a twelfth-century bridge.

After this whistle-stop tour of Stirling, a town highly praised by Scott in *Waverley*, the visitors made for the station. There, they were surprised and delighted to see a company of Highland guards in full regalia waiting for Her Majesty. The Queen had visited Edinburgh the previous day and a salute had been fired in her honour. With their striking figures, the Scottish troops looked more martial than their English counterparts, and the guards were magnificent in their dress uniforms. Their commanding officer glowed in his bright uniform as he stood with his left hand resting on the gleaming hilt of his claymore. His men did not march to trumpets, drums or fifes; instead joyful pibrochs issued from a piper's glowing instrument.[2]

The whistle blew, and soon the train was steaming for Edinburgh. Jacques constantly looked out for the royal train. A swift, noisy whoosh, and it had rushed past, without him seeing anything.

The Scottish Central Railway makes it possible to cover the journey in an hour and a quarter, despite a slight detour to Polmont Junction. From there, the train passed through Mary Queen of Scot's birthplace, Linlithgow, a small town on the edge of a lake, and sped past the ruins of Niddrie Castle, where the unfortunate queen stopped to rest after her flight from Loch Leven. The train crossed Almond Water over a viaduct of thirty-six arches and, leaving behind the Pentland Hills,[3] plunged into the Edinburgh tunnel, stopping at the General Railway Station near the Scott monument.

'First, let's have lunch,' Jacques said. 'Then we'll go to the B–s' house for our luggage. I hope we don't find it locked up.'

What better place for lunch than their little tavern on the High Street? The cold meat was reasonably good there, the bread as poor as anywhere in Britain, while the ale frothed joyfully in the metal pint mugs. After their meal, they decided to go to Inverleith Row by a roundabout route down Princes Street and Leith Walk as far as Leith. Situated at the mouth of a river bearing the same name, this busy town is Edinburgh's harbour and a small industrial centre. Leith also has its new and old towns, just like a capital city. Several ships were moored in the harbour. One of them, they were delighted to see, was flying a tricolour at a mizzen-gaff, while a tricolour pendant flapped in the wind from another mast.

'That's a French naval ship,'[4] Jacques said.

He was right. It was a sloop, whose role was to control fishing rights. On the quay where it was docked, bystanders watched its crew exercising on deck. Jacques could not resist going on board the elegant ship to shake hands with his fellow-countrymen – as if he had been six thousand leagues from home, somewhere in India or China. He asked for the captain who was not on board, but his second in command welcomed them into his cabin where, over French cigars and glasses of Sauternes, they talked about Paris and Edinburgh, discussed women from all angles and proclaimed Parisiennes the uncontested queens of the world.

After an hour of earnest talk, Jacques and Jonathan were shown round the ship. Then they visited Leith and saw the spot where, following the death of King Francis II, Mary Stuart landed on her return from France, which she would never see again. Wherever they went, they came across memories of the lovely queen, to whom it is impossible not to be indulgent.

Notes

[1] Verne drew on this paragraph for his description of Partridge, the faithful servant in *Le Rayon vert* ('The Green Ray'), chapter 2. Verne had problems with the meaning – and spelling! – of filibeg philabeg/fillebet etc (kilt), pouch and sporran. MS: *philabeg*: 'philabey'; *sporran*: 'sporrang'; for clasp he wrote 'pouch', surely a misunderstanding.

[2] *pibrochs*: On his return from Scotland, Verne wrote the lyrics for *Souvenirs d'Ecosse*, a song composed by Aristide Ignard (Jonathan) and inspired by the Highland tunes, especially pibrochs, they had heard on their journey.

[3] The Pentland Hills are in fact well to the south of the River Almond.

[4] *a French naval ship*: Jules Verne's younger brother, Paul, was a career officer in the French Navy from 1850 to 1857.

36

The London train

T HE HARBOUR JETTY of Leith extends for a mile into the sea, offering an unusual view of the Firth. After Leith, the road goes along the coast to Newhaven, where the cackle of fishwives is proverbial. From there they retraced the walk to Inverleith Row that they had taken with Miss Amelia and her parents. At the house, they found that their trunks and other items of luggage had been left in the servants' care and stood waiting in the hall. Relieved that it was safe, Jonathan agreed that they would return in the evening for the luggage. Their next step was to check the time of the train, so they returned to the General Station, the terminus for the North British Railway, and with some difficulty received confirmation that the train would be leaving at eight that evening. They had a quick dinner in the High Street and Jacques insisted on tasting mock-turtle soup, which had a calf's head instead of a turtle swimming in the spicy broth. After that, it was time to take leave of their favourite places in Edinburgh.

With heavy hearts, they walked down the Canongate one last time, waved goodbye to Holyroodhouse and returned to the cab-stand on Princes Street by way of North Bridge where a pretty girl sold them various tartan objects, such as brooches, purses, pincushions and stamp wallets, all in the various checks of the MacGregor, Macdonald, Maclean, Stuart and Colquhoun Clans. An hour later they were back at the station with their luggage and after one last sad glance at Edinburgh Castle Jacques followed his friend into the building. Passengers were besieging the ticket offices, and the employees could not handle the requests fast enough. A constant hum, dominated occasionally by shouts and yells, filled the station. With a struggle Jonathan thrust his way to a counter and asked for two seats to London. He never worked out how much he paid for them.

Jonathan counted on taking the luggage into the compartment, as they had done on the journey from Liverpool, but when he glanced in the corner where the porter had left their portmanteaux, he found they had disappeared.

'Where's our luggage?' he asked Jacques. 'I thought you were keeping an eye on it.'

Jacques blinked. Suddenly, in a dark corner, they spotted their luggage vanishing into a bottomless pit.

'It seems we must register it,' Jacques said. 'I suppose we just ask for a receipt.'

But the attendants refused to consider such an indiscreet request.

'If we ever see our trunks again, we'll be lucky,' Jonathan said. 'To think I left my passport in mine!'

It was too late to worry. A crowd was pressing towards the platform, rushing down a stone staircase like a raging torrent, carrying down heads of all shapes and sizes.

'It's the Inversnaid Falls, only noisier,' Jacques said. 'We'd better look out. We're only two tiny drops in all this water.'

Crushed and out of breath, the Parisians finally reached the long line of coaches, but most of them were full or nearly so. Jacques ran up the platform while Jonathan ran down it, looking into every doorway without finding a vacant seat. The train seemed to be overflowing. It was on the point of leaving and the Parisians' anxiety grew as they realized they could not retrieve their luggage if they did not get on. At last, just as the engine's strident whistle cut through the hubbub, Jacques spotted two empty seats in a third-class carriage. He jumped aboard, Jonathan followed, and they silenced the protests of the passengers with the universal language of fists. The train moved off, bearing a gigantic throng towards London.

This monstrous, riotous, endless train was, alas, an 'excursion' train, taking back to London a crowd of English trippers. Jacques was terrified at the thought of having to spend fifteen dreadful hours in such company.

The whole coach was in fact a single compartment in which forty passengers were packed like merchandise. The wooden seats, as soft as heart of oak, provided back-breaking repose. The tall narrow windows did not allow in enough air to meet minimum conditions of hygiene. But these were small discomforts compared with this gathering of rowdy cockneys and big intrusive John Bulls – large paunchy men, paunchy as Englishmen can be, with thick flushed heads, arrogantly scornful looks, a pretentiously sardonic manner and a coarse humour fuelled by rivers of gin and whisky; big ungainly women dressed in fashions and colours as worn as themselves; children of all ages, from the breast-suckling to the age of reason, crying, yelling, whining – such was the company on an English holiday excursion. Some were whole families: a sour couple, young misses with blank blue eyes, backward-seeming boys. And all that mob ate, slept, roared, without regard for their neighbours, with the impudence and assurance of people in their element. It was Noah's Ark with a whole menagerie of biped species, but Mount Ararat was still a long way off.

'Well, if these are the nation's cotton lords and merchant princes, I don't think much of them,' Jacques told his friend. 'When one is landed in such company, the only thing to do is to sleep. So – good night!'

37

Old King Coal

It is even harder to sleep on a wooden bench when one shrinks from leaning one's head on a fellow-passenger's shoulder. Even so, Jacques succeeded in withdrawing from the din and dozing with his head resting on his hat box. He woke now and then with a crick in his back and cramps in his legs to push away his massive neighbour who was crushing him. He felt the train hurtling him through the night at a dizzy speed, unchecked by a single stop between Edinburgh and London. The railway-line headed towards the coast and crossed the Scottish border at Berwick to enter Northumberland. Jonathan could not sleep and at Newcastle,[1]

The kingdom of coal was ablaze. (p. 162)

The land of fire vanished in the dark. (p. 162)

through a half-open window, he glimpsed a terrifying nightscape. The kingdom of coal was ablaze. Plumes of fire flickered above the tall factory chimneys; these are the trees of this dirty black region, and they form an immense forest, illuminated by wild, tawny reflections. A low endless moan rises from the pits, where relentless burrowing takes place in the bowels of coalmines that even unravel under the sea, scorning the powerless waves. Newcastle, the city of coal, produces enough to supply the whole world and has a merchant fleet of 200000 tons.

The train pursued its nightmarish ride and the land of fire vanished in the dark. The night drew on, without lulling the unbearably rowdy trainload to sleep.

Jacques was dozing uneasily when suddenly his neighbour woke him with a blow and declared: 'It is York city.'

Jacques was so incensed he lost his temper and hurled his whole repertoire of insults at the man who listened with a blank grin to this avalanche, which exhuasted his vocabulary. Never had Jacques so much regretted not knowing English. He tried to make Jonathan swear at this insular person in his mother tongue, but the musician obstinately refused. He had resigned himself to their travelling conditions and worried only about his passport in the missing trunk.

A few hours later, the sun was rising over the Duchy of Leicester. A few ancient remains, half-Saxon, half-Norman, were visible in a fertile land of wide, lush meadows where great oxen, the pride and consolation of English stomachs, lay absorbing the morning dew. Cottages appeared in the pleasant scenery, and long rows of small houses, all democratically identical, stretched along neat roads. A thin mist blurred the regular lines of the landscape, creating a special light.

Dawn brought renewed noise and activity in the compartment. Smelly edibles emerged from hidden depths, bottles were uncorked and a mixture of raw spirits and ripe pork laced the heated air. Jacques found the effluvia all the more unpleasant since he was hungry and thirsty, with no hope of a remedy. He tried to open a window, but met unanimous opposition. They were obviously the kind of people who could travel in a sweat-house and enjoy it.

In these conditions, the journey seemed endless and it would have been unbearable but for the young men's interest in people and society. After a long night of noise and insomnia faces were coming into focus at last, each with its own expression. Many of the passengers had travelled to Edinburgh for pleasure. Others, however, were taking advantage of the cheap fare to emigrate – or immigrate – with their pinched families, taking with them their few possessions in ragged tartans and in parcels fastened with headscarves. Yet another trainload of misery for the capital!

Slowly the scenery changed. Lanes became streets, villages suburbs. The air thickened and darkened. Factory chimneys generously belched their share of smoke and soot into the grimy sky. The railway-line alternately passed over long streets and plunged through sinister tunnels, stopping at last in a station. Jonathan leaped out and ran to ask about his luggage. A hill of packages and a mountain of luggage appeared on the platform, everything mixed up, crushed, upside down. Owing to a special law of gravity, large pieces of luggage sat on small ones, heavy ones on flimsy ones, with cardboard boxes flattened beneath the rest. There was no-one in charge and people just helped themselves to whatever suited them. Jonathan finally succeeded in recovering his misshapen property and, without asking for second helpings, he and Jacques jumped into one of the cabs which waited inside the station. A few minutes later, after a journey of 395 miles completed in 15 hours, our friends were leaving the Northern Railway Station and crossing New Road.

Note

[1] In chapter 10 of *Vingt mille lieues sous les mers* ('Twenty Thousand Leagues Under the Sea'), Captain Nemo refers to underwater mines like the ones described here.

38

London Bridge

THE YOUNG PARISIANS asked the cabby to drive them to London Bridge and Family Hotel, which the B– family had recommended. It was conveniently near the station where they would be catching a train to Brighton and hence to France. The two young men were given a big dark room at the top of one of those confusing English staircases. The room had two big beds with white curtains. As they cleaned themselves up, Jacques said:

'The *Richard* guidebook and others suggest compressed tours of London – but even for the briefest tour they recommend at least five days.[1] We can spare only two days, so we'll have to whizz around.'

The young Parisians asked the cabby to drive them to London Bridge. (p. 165)

'Which means there's no time to waste. But let's go to the post-office first to see if there are any letters waiting.'

Jacques had a plan of the city and he studied it carefully before they set out.[2]

They crossed back over London Bridge, which was incredibly busy. There were four lines of traffic: omnibuses, cabs, broughams, carriages, drays, waggons, barrows, carts – vehicles of all kinds heading for every possible destination – and splendid horses in gleaming harnesses. The pavements were crowded with silent, preoccupied people, all in a hurry.

It is useless to try crossing from one pavement to the other here. The traffic makes this impossible for several hours a day. London Bridge is the last one before the Thames estuary – seagoing ships stop there, with only steamboats and barges operating upstream – and it is understandable that this link between the City and south London should be so crowded. Jacques was astonished by the flow of vehicles, yet they represented only a fraction of the capital's 3000 omnibuses and 4000 cabs.

To the right, the Thames was blotted out by steamers moored outside the docks and bound for every continent. To the left the wide river was crowded with forty or fifty little steamboats, *watermen*, plying up and down without colliding or getting in each other's way. As the boats approached the embankments, their impatient passengers did not all wait for the gangways to be brought in from the quayside: they jumped overboard, landing on the quayside like a troupe of clowns vaulting over a circus horse.

In five granite strides over the Thames, London Bridge reaches the top of King William Street. A short distance away, the Monument raises its high fluted column 'of the Italo Vitruvian Doric order', as the English like to say. This column supports a burning urn and it was built on the spot where the Great Fire of 1666 stopped after reducing much of the city to ashes – Jacques recalled a magnificent description of the Fire in the anonymous novel, *Whitefriars*.[3] The Monument soon came to be used principally by people wishing to hurl their depressed selves into empty space; to kill off this fashion, the authorities enclosed the balcony at the top of the column in an iron cage so that people could admire the view without jumping overboard. Since then, of course, no-one bothers climbing to the top. People tell the story of a worthy businessman who, finding his affairs had taken an awkward turn, arrived on the platform with the intention of throwing himself off on the very day it was being caged in. Unable to commit suicide as planned he returned to his offices, tried his luck at speculation once again and became a millionaire several times over. He now finds the cage very attractive at the top of the column. No-one else does.

A succession of long streets led Jacques and Jonathan from William Street to the post-office, cutting across the heart of the City where even small shops look like stores and shopkeepers like managers. The activity in this area is intense. One sees no idlers in the streets, only men who look as if they can set up a limited company in anything with a capital of several million pounds. One meets neither young nor middle aged nor old Londoners – only dealers: cotton lords, wool dukes, brown sugar marquises, candle barons; a whole array of merchant princes and nabobs hurry to mysterious little offices and secret rooms where they get through the day's business before returning to luxurious mansions on

The activity in this area is intense. (p.167)

Regent Street or Belgrave Square. True, in this bustling capital where poverty is as absolute as wealth, millionaires rub shoulders unaffectedly with nihilionaires; and if a rich man does not toss banknotes to the poor, it is only because they can't give him any change.

The General Post Office is a Grecian temple with a portico of Doric columns. Time has already left its sooty stratum on the ribs of the building's entablature and on the sculptures of its pediment. Without pausing to examine the building in detail, Jacques and Jonathan made for the *poste restante* counter, where they were told there were no letters for them. The next urgent task was to find some lunch. In the dimly-lit room of an unassuming tavern they found seats between two cubicles of dark mahogany. A distinguished-looking waiter in black came to their table, followed shortly afterwards by single plates containing a tiny fraction of the 250 000 oxen and 1 700 000 sheep which the Gargantuan capital devours each year. Two pints followed, mere drops in the 43 000 000 gallons of ale that quench its thirst each year.

Meanwhile, busy people succeeded each other at neighbouring tables, lunching off the *Times* or the *Morning Chronicle* and a few drops of lightly-sugared tea served in microscopic cups.

The tourists walked towards Saint Paul's, whose dome surveyed the scene above the line of surrounding rooftops. (p. 168)

'How can that keep them going until dinner?' Jacques asked. 'I feel sorry for them.'

After a more substantial meal than their neighbours, the tourists left the table and walked towards Saint Paul's, whose dome surveyed the scene above the line of surrounding rooftops.

Notes

[1] *Richard*: Jean-Baptiste Richard, engineer, geographer and author of guidebooks on France and other European countries.

[2] For the descriptions of London in this and the following chapters, Verne borrowed from Francis Wey's *Les Anglais chez eux* (*Musée des familles*, December 1850) ('A Frenchman sees the English in the Fifties', adapted by V Pirie, London, 1935).

[3] *Whitefriars* refers to *Whitefriars or the Days of Charles the Second*, an historical romance, London 1844 (possibly by Emma Robinson).

39

St Paul's and the Thames

S T PAUL'S IS AN INCOMPLETE imitation of St Peter's in Rome. More massive than beautiful, the present cathedral stands on the site of Inigo Jones's splendid Gothic cathedral¹ which was destroyed by the fire in 1666. Externally, the architecture of St Paul's is entirely ruled by the Corinthian order. A forest of columns soars up to support the dome. The outside of the building is black with soot, but projections and ledges exposed to the north wind present large patches of white shade, light and shadow being inverted. This produces a strange effect of symmetrical strata of snowdrifts on the profiles of entablatures, fillets of columns and acanthus leaves of capitals. Pleasantly solid, the bell tower and clock tower rise to either side of the porch, but the golden fir-cones at the top produce an inelegant effect. The outer walls of the cathedral are 37 metres high, but the sense of height is diminished by the overall massiveness of the building. An attractive gallery crowns the entablature supported by the columns of the dome, and the cupola is topped by a lantern, itself surrounded by a second gallery. The ball and cross rise a further thirty-seven metres above this gallery.

Jacques had obtained these exact measurements, but typically refused to believe them. Overcoming his friend's reluctance, and despite their tight schedule and general weariness, he insisted on climbing up into the dome as far as he could. Like many of England's religious buildings, St Paul's is surrounded by a cemetery which was recently still operating – as businessmen would say. In the past few years, however, financial companies have been set up to create cemeteries in London. The oldest, Kensal Green Cemetery Company, does flourishing business and its shares are probably quoted on the London Exchange, where everyone must tremble when they rise.

On entering the cathedral, Jacques and Jonathan were struck by its cold luminosity and grandiose austerity. There were no paintings, only a few ridiculous monuments and tasteless statues honouring the memory of great men. After an indifferent glance at this indoor necropolis, Jacques headed for the door leading to the dome. There, for one shilling and sixpence, he obtained the right to go up to the lantern. A spiralling wooden staircase took the two climbers to an inner gallery which encircles the base of the dome. This is called the whispering gallery. A little man who has grown old in this honourable profession went to the opposite side of it and whispered. His whisper rushed back to their startled ears like a hurricane.[2] At last daylight flowed in through a window and they saw the gallery of the entablature.

The view would be excellent from there if the eternal fog did not obscure the horizon. On a fine day, one can trace the Thames from the docks to Westminster Palace although the Parliament towers can more often be sensed than seen. Around the base of St Paul's sprawls a pleasing cluster of buildings, from which spring forth the countless spires of three hundred churches which dot the area like pawns on a huge chessboard, St Paul's being the king and Westminster Tower the queen.

After viewing the city by the dull light of an English sun that seemed to be shining through frosted glass, Jacques dragged Jonathan up a narrow corkscrew staircase that led them to the lantern gallery. There, after

They were soon walking down from London Bridge along the Thames.
(p. 171)

handing their hats to attendants whom Jonathan called the lantern's Higher Officers, they climbed up a kind of ladder to the ball, up which they scrambled, clinging with hands and feet to the hummocks and hollows of the bronze. Jonathan did not make it to the top, unlike his bold companion who scrambled up to the bowl, which is two metres across. Up to eight people can squeeze in there.

There, straddling the metal bar that serves as axis for the dome, Jacques told Jonathan:

'Now or never the place to remind you, in the manner of Stendhal, of the heights of some famous buildings. St Peter's of Rome, 411 feet; Strasburg cathedral, 426 feet; the Great Pyramid, 438 feet; the spire of Les Invalides, in Paris, 324 feet; while this bowl I'm perched in is poised 319 feet above the pavements of London.[3] And now I can come down.'

They were soon walking down from London Bridge along the Thames. The stone steps leading down to landing-stages were crowded with groups of half-naked children asking for alms by selling matches and chemical tinder. The two friends boarded one of those swift steamboats crowded with passengers which for a penny fare plied between London Bridge and Westminster. Equipped like the other river ferries with an excellent oscillating engine which started up immediately, the *Citizen* moved off, passing the *Sun* which was coming downstream. Standing on the capstan and using the opening and closing of his hands, the master on board signalled instructions to a child who communicated them to the mechanic in a shrill, high-pitched voice. After a ringing 'go ahead',[1] the steamer turned upstream.

The absence of quaysides gives the Thames a bizarre appearance. Depots, gasometers, wharfs, factories and warehouses press along the banks, opening straight onto the river so that ships can load and unload cargo directly. Many of these buildings are decorated with high towers; some advertise their purpose in large lettering of all styles. After lowering its jointed funnel to a third of its normal height, the *Citizen* passed under the huge cast-iron archways of Southwark Bridge and Blackfriars Bridge. It slipped past the Temple's cool inviting gardens which contain Anglo-Saxon monuments, and continued towards Somerset House, a handsome Venetian palace sheltering the Stamp Office, the Royal Mint and the Public Records. Seen from the middle of the river, it is an impressive building. Time and damp have eroded the arches of its lower arcades and impregnated them with artificial age. With its nine splendid arches supporting a straight roadway, Waterloo Bridge stretched out its elegant profile over twelve hundred feet. Built in Cornish granite, it looks indestructible. Well beyond it, an airy suspension bridge boldly spanned the Thames then, after a bend in the river, the old bridge of Westminster came into sight, half of it already replaced by a superb-looking new iron bridge. The *Citizen* had reached its destination and the moment it docked, Jacques and Jonathan dashed on to the embankment to admire the façade of the new Houses of Parliament.

Notes

[1] Inigo Jones (1573–1651) built several of England's stately homes.
[2] The whispering gallery inspired fictional devices in Verne's later work, whereby characters could communicate over a distance by means of conductive materials (*Voyage au centre de la Terre* ('Journey to the centre of the Earth'), chapter 28 and *Mathias Sandorff*, Part I, chapter 5).
[3] Stendhal gives these details in *Promenades dans Rome* (entry for 12 June 1828) in *Voyage en Italie*. (Paris, Pléiade, 1984, pp 870–1).
[4] *Go a head* (sic) is the name given to an airship by the members of the Weldon Institute in *Robur-le-Conquérant* ('Clipper of the Clouds') (chapter 2).

40

Westminster, Whitehall and Trafalgar Square

JACQUES WAS BOWLED OVER by the efflorescent style of the Houses of Parliament, which set him raving about the 'rich ornamentation, tapestry of royal blazons, lacework of chiselled reliefs, intricate embroidery on friezes, architraves and cornices'. Here indeed was 'a flowering of the whole botanical Renaissance, a veil of Brussels lace draped over a gigantic building' – what might be called the Anglo-Saxon millionaire style.

Although the new Palace of Westminster was inaugurated only recently, in 1847, it seems to belong to the world of fairy-tales. The building has several soaring towers. One, with a pointed steeple, presents to the four sides of London the four faces of its gigantic clock. Another, Victoria Tower, rises as high as St Paul's and although impressively massive, it is chiselled from top to bottom with a goldsmith's delicacy and effectively decorated with coats of arms and heraldic emblems. The façade overlooking the square is irregular, wings jut out here and there, displaying the flamboyant wealth of their Gothic windows. The riverside front, a thousand feet in length, is simply perfect. The profusion of detail may detract from the majesty of the whole, but one cannot fail to be moved by this tropical vegetation which has blossomed in the mists of England. It is hard to wrench oneself away from this magnificent sight and it impresses even those who have criticized it as just an immense mass of sculptures. The palace is a precious reliquary, a gigantic medieval casket – a fairy dream translated into priceless stone by the world's most industrial people.

Externally, Westminster Abbey presents a frigid contrast to this Renaissance extravagance. Built in the late Gothic style, it is depressingly black, while the inside is a vast necropolis crowded with inelegant tombs and allegorical figures which make the beholder want to laugh. Jacques and Jonathan shrugged at the self-glorifying bas-reliefs which private citizens can have installed in the Abbey if they pay the right price.

Protestant churches do not honour the saints of early Christianity but men whose wealth buys them immortality. Truly memorable, though, is the Poets' Corner where a fine, inspired sculpture of Shakespeare stands out among the statues and busts of Milton, Addison, Dryden, Gray, Goldsmith, Butler, Spenser and Garrick. The chapels in the choir contain famous tombs: here lie Edward's two children, there Mary Queen of Scots and Elizabeth, reconciled for eternity – the sight of their two tombstones in the same chapel is a moving one. In the apse is the Henry VII chapel, a marvellous jewel in stone to which no words can do justice – this flawless masterpiece of Renaissance art is the work of Benvenuto Cellini.

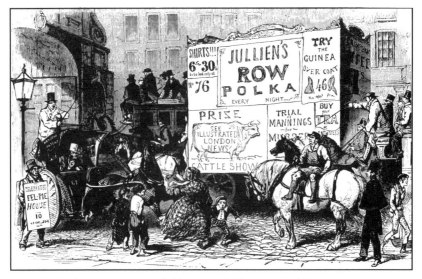

The two Frenchmen were surrounded by a crowd of beggars. (p. 174)

On emerging from the cathedral, with its mishmash of architectural marvels and absurdities, the two Frenchmen were surrounded by a crowd of beggars selling prints and descriptions of London's monuments. They found it difficult to be rid of them and Jacques did not have the heart to deny a few pence to the eager sweepers who cleaned the pavement before his feet. English begging is an exercise in ingenuity – in its own way a form of trade and speculation.

They walked down Parliament Street past Whitehall, a palace with dread associations even though it has been rebuilt since Charles I was executed. It is now a medium-sized building decorated with Ionic columns.

'There's no need and no time to linger here discussing the window which overlooks the king's scaffold,' Jacques said.

'That's very good of you,' Jonathan said. The pace of their excursion had already exhausted him. 'Where are we?'

'At Charing Cross, where royal coronations used to take place. This is Trafalgar Square. According to my plan, that's the National Gallery on the far side. It's such an ugly building it can't be anything else – and that's being polite. Do you see Nelson's statue perched on top of that Doric column? The great sailor has a lightning conductor going from one end of him to the other. It's typical of the great English people's sense of fairness to raise a statue to Nelson for his victories of Aboukir and Trafalgar, but to impale him for his private crimes. We shall now leave this dull sloping square for St James's Park and rest our eyes on some greenery, with a quick glance at the clubs on Pall Mall on the way.'

Each club is a small palace. No other country has buildings of this kind which are so distinguished. There are many of them in London, but the Pall Mall and United Service clubs, the Italian-style Conservative Club, and the Athenaeum are outstanding.[1] One should not, of course, be surprised that London is so rich in monuments: the city has ninety-one corporations – ranging from haberdashers, drapers and fishmongers to goldsmiths, furriers and publicans – each with its seat, a huge assembly room and charitable centres to help members who fall on hard times. There are also some forty scientific societies of every imaginable type with their headquarters, complete with columns and pediments. There are as many clubs as societies; each of them spreads itself out, squares its shoulders or casually reclines, providing custom and inspiration for English architects and multiplying the capital's number of interesting buildings.

'And now,' Jacques said, 'let's go down the steps of Waterloo Place to Horse Guards Parade. You'll see the Duke of York's column. You can go up it for sixpence – or free if you are under three.'

'What would I do up there at the age of two-and-a-half?' Jonathan asked.

'I don't know, but such is the rule. It reminds me of a notice in the omnibuses back home. "Children aged under three can travel free provided they stay on their knees". That's how they put things in Nantes.'

Note

1. In *Le Tour du monde en quatre-vingt jours* ('Around the World in Eighty Days'), Verne makes Phileas Fogg a member of the Reform Club, whose members are shown gathered at St Paul's in an illustration of Francis Wey's *Les Anglais chez eux* ('A Frenchman sees the English in the Fifties', adapted by V Pirie, London, 1935). (*Musée des familles*, December 1850).

41

West End travels

THE SQUARE AT THE BACK of the Horse Guards is used as a regimental parade ground, and every morning one may hear bands playing the tunes that would be catcalled in Paris cafés. The two tourists arrived too late for Jonathan to hear English variations on some theme from *Il Trovatore*, but St James's Park offered them a stroll over fine lawns and along shaded paths. A little river crosses the park but is spoilt by a heavy, graceless suspension bridge. North of the Park, St James's Palace, of little architectural interest, is used for official ceremonies, receptions and royal events. At the far end of the park stands Buckingham Palace, the residence of Queen Victoria. The main façade provides few clues as to the overall style and ornamentation of the palace, but the wing overlooking the royal family's private gardens is reputed to be attractive. Adjoining and continuing St James's Park is Green Park where nice little sheep nibble a broad expanse of city grass and can imagine themselves in open country. London butchers pay for

Hyde Park is an immense garden. (p. 178)

177

the right to graze sheep there. On the whole, London's pleasant, useful, relaxing parks are only casually tended, but in the heart of this huge city their unenclosed lawns are open to all who wish to stroll there.

At the far end of Green Park rise the Triumphal Arch and the monumental entrance to Hyde Park. Jacques pointed to the equestrian statue on the platform of the arch, asking:

'Have you ever seen anything uglier, more ridiculous or in worse taste? The horse looks drunk. Its rider is the Duke of Wellington, whose house you see here. The old hero could see himself from his own dining-room and he must have been truly heroic if it didn't put him off his food. But so that he could see himself from his bedroom too, the ladies of London had another statue of him erected on the edge of Hyde Park, representing him as a gigantic Achilles. I can't imagine why they chose that troublemaker from antiquity who owed his reputation for courage to no personal merit. Worse, though, poor Wellington stands there in the nude, a stone nudity that makes you shiver!' He added: 'The whole country swarms with statues, busts and portraits of Wellington. They have exploited him the way they exploited Waterloo.'

Hyde Park is an immense garden with wide drives, vast lawns, splendid trees, a respectable river and a magnificent stone bridge. It is a fashionable society meeting-place. Family carriages are banned but there are many other horse-drawn vehicles, mostly driven by members of the 'Four in Hand Club' who claim to be the world's best drivers.

Jonathan enjoyed the glimpses of English daily life. (p. 180)

*Jacques was amazed by the number of cobblers and dressmakers there seemed
to be in the city. (p. 180)*

During the season, when all the gentry and nobility return to the city
from the country, the Hyde Park crowd of pedestrians and riders is a
curious one. Whole families – father, mother, sons and daughters –
gallop by on valuable horses. Old lords bring their boredom for its daily
constitutional before taking it for a doze to Westminster where ushers
nudge them awake to cast their vote. One also meets charming
Englishwomen. In Hyde Park, as in the nation as a whole, men tend to
be outnumbered by the fair sex. This, Jonathan observed, was bound to
imperil England in a none-too-distant future.

'Which means,' Jacques said, embroidering on his friend's comment,
'that there's no shortage of old maids on this island, so if you wish to

179

treat yourself to a rich heiress anxious to be rid of her celibacy, you'll have no problem. Do you see the coats of arms on all those vehicles? Every time you see one emblazoned with a lozenge, it means there's a daughter ripe for picking.'

'I'm too exhausted to worry about that,' Jonathan said, 'and time is rather short. My main concern at the moment is to find somewhere to sit and rest.'

'No! Keep walking! Come on! But when we get out of the park, we'll find a cab and go to our little alehouse for dinner.'

The tavern was a long way off, but during their walk through the city they had not found a single restaurant. There was no shortage of boarding-houses and eating-houses, but they looked so dismal, so lifeless or so shut in on themselves that the idea of crossing their thresholds never entered their minds.

The cab they found was driven by a very distinguished-looking fellow – every inch the English peer. He drove them down Piccadilly, a wide street lined with low, irregular houses, many of them with black façades, yet suggestive of ease and comfort. Each family lives in a separate house, with a wide balcony supported on an openwork iron platform. Considering the current fashion for crinolines, this could be a source of embarrassment, but neither the Englishwomen on their balconies nor the Englishmen in the street below give them a second look. It is easy to understand how, with everyone living in a private house, London should have 200 000 of them sprawling over 12 000 streets. Mr Horace Say[1] was right when he declared that London was not a city but a province covered with houses.

In the elegant quarters of Piccadilly, Regent Street and Haymarket, one finds the same animation as in the City, though it is more relaxed. Jonathan enjoyed the glimpses of English daily life observed as they crossed Mayfair and approached the Strand. A postman wearing a red uniform knocked twice at private houses, two dry knocks on a little knocker. Honourable gentlemen announced themselves with five slow knocks while elegant women gave seven hurried little knocks. Thus one knew what kind and quality of caller to expect. Jacques, for his part, was amazed by the number of cobblers and dressmakers there seemed to be in the city – thousands, by his estimate! As for cigar-vendors, whose trade is uncontrolled, they are innumerable but, despite their enticing slogans and placards, their cigars are rubbish.

After crossing Trafalgar Square, the cab drove past an old Anglo-Saxon-style building full of character: the home of the Duke of Northumberland. In one of the drawing-rooms hangs a framed banknote for 500 000 francs which the duke has the cheek to describe as an old master.

Advertising has become an epidemic
fever in England. (p. 181)

The Strand is one long shopping street linking Westminster and the City. It bustles with activity; walls, housefronts and even pavements are covered with slogans and posters of all kinds, while sandwich-men walk up and down encased in cones or pyramids that appeal to desire and greed. Advertising has become an epidemic fever in England.

Note

[1] Author of *De l'Angleterre et des Anglais* (Paris and London, 1815) ('England and the English', London 1816).

42

Jacques and Jonathan at the theatre

NDER THE COACHMAN'S SKILFUL guidance, the cab cut swiftly through the heavy traffic, an unending flow of brightly-coloured vehicles, some strangely designed. After driving past the Doric façade of Somerset House, they reached Temple Bar, the last vestige of the old city boundary: it is a gateway resembling a triumphal arch, always open, except to her Gracious Majesty the Queen when she chooses to visit this part of London. In order to enter, she must obtain the permission of the Lord Mayor, and when she wears the Crown Jewels, which are kept in the Tower, she must give the Lord Mayor a receipt for them; for those jewels belong to the British nation, to the blank-eyed beggars who slink past with starving stomachs, and the dead-drunk sailors who stagger outside gin-houses.

'In the old days,' Jacques said, 'they used to display the heads of executed criminals on that gate. I've been told that on public holidays they decorate it with cardboard heads, perfect imitations, looking as bloody as John Bull's roast-beef.'

'I can easily believe that,' Jonathan said. 'What a crowd! Here is Ludgate Hill and there's the dome of St Paul's. The street's swarming with urchins! You'd think this was Liverpool.'

'I think it's the same all over England,' Jacques said. 'That may be why, having all these lively urchins around, English novelists like to trace their heroes' lives from their tenderest infancy up.'

There were many churches in that part of London, but the Parisians did not have enough time to visit them. Most of them looked shut anyway. A noticeboard affixed to the door and protected behind wire-netting gave the parish minister's name, his address and the sort of business he indulged in with his wife and pretty children.

Down Fleet Street and the Old Bailey, where the nameplates were as hard to make out as in most streets, the two Frenchmen reached Newgate Prison, recently built, but still a dark, forbidding building:

Princess's Royal Theatre
Oxford street

under the management of Mr. A. Harris, Pubham place, Brumpton.

Last six nights of the season.

On Monday, sept. 2, & During the Week
Shakespeare's tragedy of

Macbeth !

with Locke's music.

Duncan (King of Scotland)		Mr. Garden
Malcolm	(his sons)	Mr. J.-G. Shore
Donalbain		Miss Woodward

Macbeth	Generals of the King's army	Mr. James Anderson
Banquo		Mr. Fernandez

Macduff		Mr. Basil Potter
Lennox		Mr. R. Cathiart
Ross	(noblemen of Scotland)	Mr. Raymond
Menteith		Mr. Richardson
Angus		Mr. Andrews
Caithness		Mr. Wilson

Fleance (son to Banquo)	Miss Denvil
Siward (Earl of Northumberland)	Mr. Hastings
Seton (an officer attending on Macbeth)	Mr. Paulo

Physician, Mr. Harcourt   Wounded officer Mr. Dawson
Officers, Mr. J. Collett, Mr. Dahy, etc.
Apparitions, Mr. Johnston, Miss B. Adams, Miss A. Denvil

Lady Macbeth	Miss Elsworthy
Gentlewoman (attending on Lady Macbeth)	Miss Leclercq
Hecate	Mr. Bartleman

Witches, Mr. Franck Malthews, Mr. T.H. Higgie, Mr. H. Saker
Singing Witches, Miss Rebecca Isaac, cond. Mr. Rayner

Act l
Camp near Fores. Site of Sweno's pillar. A Heath.
A room in Macbeth's castle at Inverness. Exterior of same.

Act ll
Court within Macbeth's castle at Inverness.

Act lll
Landscape, near Inverness. Chamber in the palace of Fores.
Glen near the palace.
Banqueting hall in the palace.

Act IV
The pit of Acheron
Exterior of an Anglo-saxon city, with Roman Wall

Act V
Chamber within Macbeth's castle at Dunsniane.
Court of the castle
Country near Dunsniane. View near the castle.
Outer Walls of the castle.

to conclude with the farce of

The First Night

Achille Talma Dufard	Mr. A. Harris
The Honorable Bertie Fitzdaugh	Mr. T.-H. Higgie
Hyacinth Parnassus	Mr. R. Cathiart
Theophilus Vamp	Mr. Collett
Timotheus Flat	Mr. Garden
Miss Arabella Fitzjames	Miss Rose Leclercq
Emilie Antoinette Rose	Miss Maria Harris

(pupil of Mrs Selby) her seventh appearance on any stage.

in the course of the Evening,
Waltz, « Cupid's Ladder »   Montgomery

Saturday next ; september 14th,
for the Benefit of Mr. James Anderson
and last night of the company's performing the season.

Dress circle, 5s. Boxes, 4s. Pit, 2s. Gallery, 1s.
Orchestra stalls, 6s. Private boxes, £ 2 s. 6 d £2 2 s. & £1 11s. 6 d.
Doors open at Half past Six, the performance to commence at Seven.

The accredited agents for the Sale of Boxes and Stalls : Mistissale,
Royal Library, and Hookham, Old Bond St. ; Sand, Saint-
James street ; Leader and Cock, Chappelle, and Subb, New Bond
street ; Ebbers, Old Bond street ; Cramer and Beak, and
Hammond, Regent street ; Carter, 12, Regent street ; and Keith,
Bowles and Co ; Cheapside.
The Box Office Open from 11 until a quarter to 5 o'clock daily.

Jonathan chose two seats in the stalls. (p. 187)

English architects excel at giving their buildings local colour and atmosphere. They pursued their route as far as the Bank and the Royal Exchange, both of which possess undistinguished pseudo-Graeco-Roman features. The Bank of England seems to guard itself, without that cohort of soldiers and pensioners who watch over its Paris equivalent. The Royal Exchange looks like a church – appropriately, for is it not the leading temple of those who believe in trade and speculation?

'The English have an odd way of talking about financial speculators,' Jacques said. 'They call them bears and bulls. Bold, confident, enterprising buyers are bulls. Pessimists who invariably think all is lost, the sellers in other words, are miserable cornered bears, whom the bulls send climbing for refuge into the trees. I find this animal imagery appropriate.'

After failing to salute yet another equestrian statue of Wellington and spending a few seconds (which seemed a long time) contemplating the

Lord Mayor's six Corinthian columns, they returned to their little tavern where the same distinguished-looking waiter served them a quick but scanty meal. Jacques had already planned their evening: he proposed to see *Macbeth*, which was being performed at the Princess Theatre in Oxford Street. So they jumped into an omnibus, after first working out their destination among the thousand names which decorated the signs. At half past seven they were outside the Princess Royal Theatre. Jonathan chose two seats in the stalls which cost six shillings each. As they entered the foyer, they were given a programme (like the one on pp. 184–5).

It was a medium-sized theatre, but dainty and newly decorated. Jacques found himself sitting next to elegant women in evening gowns with flowers in their hair and necklines plunging to the depths that necklines can plunge to with impunity in England. The frontage, he decided, was quite delightful. It was not yet a full house but it would fill up after nine o'clock, when seats were sold at half price.

In England, where enterprise is free, anyone may open a theatre, start an omnibus service, start a dance-hall or a cabaret, or publish a newspaper; the last is a thriving sector, since the English have 781 dailies and 480 magazines and literary reviews. The result of this unrestrained freedom means that theatre managers can do as they wish and change programmes and admission charges at will, since they alone decide how best to draw the public.

43

Lady Macbeth

T HE PLAY BEGAN. To Jacques, who did not understand a single word, it was like being at a noisy pantomine. Jonathan grasped a few words here and there, but lost track of the dialogue as he tried to understand what they meant. The acting was conventional, in a lively, romantic style, and the actors, while striving to convey the great dramatist's intent, sometimes let out dreadful yells. Most of the audience seemed to appreciate the actors' stiff, affected English manner, their exaggerations and dramatic gasps. The fighting between Macbeth and the Scottish nobility recalled a circus act, with the king carefully keeping time as he struck his foe

As Lady Macbeth, Miss Elsworthy seemed more sober and restrained. (p. 190)

Macduff, who stood by patiently waiting for him to finish before returning the blows.

As Lady Macbeth, Miss Elsworthy seemed more sober and restrained. Her acting was almost natural in contrast with the other players' romantic extravagance. The choirs were successful and the three witches screeched in bloodcurdling counterpoint to Locke's music which delighted Jonathan.

The stage-sets were simply painted and designed, and swiftly changed between each scene. To Jacques's delight some of them depicted Scottish landscapes near Inverness, superimposing recollections of his journey on their dramatic interest.

Did the actors respect Shakespeare's original text? Did they tone down the poet's blunt realism to satisfy polite English convention or did they respect its brutal splendour? This was a difficult question to answer, but one that fascinated Jacques. On the French stage the play is always abridged and mutilated, but he had read translations of *Macbeth* and knew the play well. He therefore reminded Jonathan of the famous scene in the second act, following Duncan's murder, when Macduff asks the Porter what three things drink provokes.[1] When the moment arrived, however, Jonathan listened hard but failed to understand. The doorkeeper's reply provoked general laughter in the audience.

'Bravo!' Jacques exclaimed. 'They are faithful to Shakespeare and put art before prudery. Bravo!'

'What would be scandalous,' Jonathan said, 'would be to amend Shakespeare instead of respecting his text. These worthy Englishmen are right. You must either be faithful to Shakespeare or leave him alone.'

Poorly acted, the great play was weakly applauded; English audiences tend to be restrained. Montgomery's Waltz filled the interval, without anyone listening, and the curtain soon rose for the farce which rounded off the evening.

In the first scene, Jacques immediately recognized *The First Night*: it was a translation of *Le père de la débutante*, with the theatre manager in the part of Achille Talma Dufard.[2] He acted with great brio, improvising countless additions to the original, speaking half in French, half in English, and a little bit in Italian; and, for no clear reason, Latin, even quoting the opening line of Virgil's *Georgics*.[3] The two friends held their sides in helpless laughter as they heard him declaim:

Tightiree, tyoo paytyooligh raykyoobance syub tegminay fargee.

It had never occurred to Jacques before that Latin could sound so different in an English mouth. The performance was brisk and the theatre manager's daughter, Miss Maria Harris, shared the applause with him.

Exhausted, stiff and falling asleep on their feet, the two tourists left the theatre at eleven o'clock. What a day, after the train journey they'd had!

They tottered down Regent Street in search of a cab. The streets were nearly deserted when in Paris at the same time they would have been crowded and brightly-lit. The shops here, closed since eight o'clock, provided no propitious light. Only occasionally did a ray shine through the dim glass of some alehouse or whisky-shop. Policemen moved mysteriously down the pavements, close to the wall, with small lanterns fastened to their belts, pausing at each door to check it was locked. When from time to time two or more of them met, they exchanged a few whispered words and vanished in different directions.

In Haymarket the mood changed from silence to noise, from deserted streets to animated motion. Hundreds of women wearing indescribable garments haunted one side of the broad street, practising their redoubtable profession with a sense of freedom, boldness and provocation that feared nothing from the police. This was their peak trading-time, their stock exchange, and they seemed to sell their goods as shrewdly as bankers. There was a lot of competition that evening; supply was greater than demand, and discounts were clearly offered to potential dealers.

Among those women there were many girls still young yet already withered by a dissolute life, many once-pretty creatures who had lost their fresh looks in public houses where love is rinsed in gin and brandy; for those businesses stay open until dawn, providing drinks and couches for the stupefied courtesans of Haymarket.

Nearer the Thames, down narrow, muddy alleys, the same quantity is available, though not the quality. Scenes of drunkenness and debauchery are interspersed with fights and even murders.

Repelled by disgusting scenes, Jacques and Jonathan finally found a cab which drove them back to the London Bridge Hotel, where they sank into the sleep of exhaustion, which is even deeper than the sleep of innocence.

Notes

[1] 'Nose-painting, sleep and urine'.

[2] *Le père de la débutante* is a vaudeville in five acts. The work of Bayard and Théaulon, it was first produced at the Théâtre des Variétés on 28 October, 1837.

[3] The line is in fact from the *Bucolics*, not the *Georgics:* 'Tityre, tu patulae recubans sub tegmine fagi' (O Tityrus, reclining in the shelter of the spreading beech).

44

A boat-trip on the Thames

THE NEXT MORNING, Jacques shook Jonathan awake.
'Come on, this is our last day. We're the Wandering Jews of tourism, forced by duty, not pleasure, to walk and look and look and look again. That should be our motto, don't you think?'

'Talking of mottoes,' Jonathan said, 'have you noticed that most cities and orders have them in French? You find 'Dieu et mon droit' on the national coat of arms, while the Order of the Garter has 'Honni soit qui mal y pense'.'

'Yes. It's odd.'

'Not at all. It dates from the Norman conquest. These good islanders spoke our language for two centuries, remember.'

They boarded one of the boats that go down the Thames to Greenwich. (p. 194)

Soon the skyline was bristling with the 15 000 masts of ships imprisoned in the docks. (p. 194)

'You'd never guess it from their pronunciation. But, Jonathan, this conversation would be better out of doors. Let's get moving. I've drawn up our programme and we've a full day ahead of us.'

They washed and dressed quickly, and were soon ready. They left the hotel, crossed London Bridge and boarded one of the boats that go down the Thames to Greenwich. The river was crowded with liners and coasters which were taking advantage of the falling tide and hasting downstream at full steam and full sail. The Greenwich boat moved swiftly downriver.

To the left was the Custom House, a huge building with three huge Ionic porticoes decorated with columns already being gnawed into by the damp jaws of the Thames. The river water was neither muddy nor silty, it was more like a putrid overflow of sewage. The Thames is in fact a huge drain and twice a day the tide washes back into it all the city's filth which the North Sea refuses to absorb. This is a permanent source of infection and it is not surprising that, things being as they are, the plague should have ravaged London on six occasions, claiming 100 000 victims in 1665. In the heat of June and July the stench from the river is so intolerable that Parliament, half-suffocated, is forced to adjourn.

The steamboat cut through foul water so heavy and slimy it hardly foams. Soon the skyline was bristling with the 15 000 masts of ships imprisoned in the docks, but after visiting the basins of Liverpool harbour, Jacques decided he would survive if he did not see those of London, which are no more impressive. Then, in a bend in the river, a monster appeared, the *Leviathan*, which engineering expertise had finally succeeded in setting afloat.[1] To Jacques's great regret, it was no longer possible to visit that monster of the seas which can carry twenty thousand tons of vanities. It was anchored just upstream from Greenwich, where the steamboat arrived a few minutes later.

Situated about five miles downriver from London Bridge, Greenwich is a real town. After glancing briefly at the magnificent palace England has built as a hospital for its seamen, Jacques tried in vain to show Jonathan the world-famous meridian which passes through the Observatory. They then hired a rowing-boat to return to the *Leviathan* and take a look at it from all sides. They rowed upstream, past a big schooner that has been dismasted to serve as an annexe to the Seamen's Hospital. It looked small besides the *Leviathan* which towered above Jacques and Jonathan as they rowed past paddle-boxes the size of churches. It was during this nautical outing that Jonathan stupidly dipped his finger in the Thames. He was still regretting it two days later.

After rowing around that floating city, they returned to the quayside and took a second steamboat up the Thames, disembarking at a landing-stage on the left bank, near a useless marvel: the tunnel designed and built by the French engineer, Brunel.[2] They reached the entrance of the tunnel and walked down the spiralling steps of a staircase which led them down a deep well. The circular walls of the shaft were decorated with scenes from different countries, painted with the colourful enthusiasm typical of English artists. Two galleries opened out from the bottom of the well, each 400 metres long. The right one is for

In a bend in the river, a monster appeared, the Leviathan. *(p. 195)*

pedestrians who may thus, for the price of one penny, cross the Thames below its disgusting waters. The thick atmosphere of this long bowel is dreary, grim and sepulchral, despite the light from numerous gaslamps. An arcade links the two galleries and shelters stalls where one can find the most useless and expensive objects sold by the prettiest girls in the world who are reputed to be on sale too.

As Jacques and Jonathan entered the gallery, an industrious fellow at the far end started producing sounds on his cornet for the amusement of passers-by. The brass notes sounded strange in that long vault. At first they were indistinct but soon, Jonathan, who was walking ahead, suddenly stopped and grabbed his friend's arm.

'Listen!' he said.

'What is it?'

'Don't you recognize the tune?'

Activated by senseless lips, the dreadful instrument was roaring 'Ah! l'amore, l'amore on d'ardole', from *Il Trovatore*.

'Even under the Thames!' Jacques said.

'Come, let's get out before the tunnel caves in,' Jonathan said.

They returned to the lower opening of the pit, though not without

They returned to the quayside, disembarking near a useless marvel: the tunnel designed and built by Brunel. (p. 195)

having seen in one stall a tiny steam-operated machine the size of a fist, fuelled by a gasflame which set in motion the handle of a barrel-organ. Luckily, the instrument was silent: it would certainly have played more *Trovatore.*

Jacques was happy to see daylight again and, following his programme, he set off for the Tower, which was a good distance away. Not finding a cab in the area, they had to cover it on foot. Finally, after a tiring roundabout circuit and losing their way several times in the docklands maze of streets, after seeing railway-lines that passed straight over churches and houses, and watching trains hurtle past over roofs and gables, the two exhausted friends reached the Tower of London.

Notes

[1] *Leviathan* was designed by Isambard Kingdom Brunel, who also built many bridges and helped his father with the tunnel under the Thames that Verne describes further on. Mentioned by Victor Hugo in 'Pleine Mer' (*Légende des siècles*), the huge steamer was launched in 1857 and ran into heavy financial difficulties from the start. Renamed the *Great Eastern*, it shipped 10 000 emigrants to Australia. In 1865 it was equipped to lay the first transatlantic cables, under the supervision of Cyrus Field. In 1867, Jules Verne and his brother, Paul, travelled on the ship from Liverpool to New York. During the Universal Fair in Paris, the ship made regular voyages between the old and new continents. Verne described the crossing in *Une Ville flottante* ('A Floating City'). He also mentioned the *Leviathan* in the opening chapter of *Vingt mille lieues sous les mers* ('Twenty Thousand Leagues Under the Sea').

[2] The Greenwich Footway Tunnel, designed by Sir Marc Isambard Brunel; the father of Isambard Kingdom Brunel; he was born in France but settled in England.

45

The terrible tower

SUPPOSEDLY BUILT BY William the Conqueror, the Tower is the very embodiment of the English spirit, with its traditions, its attachment to customs, its love of the past. The citadel's main curiosity lies in its warders who wear a traditional costume with coats of arms emblazoned on their chests and ribbons in their hats. Jonathan was delighted to see these characters operate; they had obviously just stepped out of the reigns of Richard III and Henry VIII to describe the bloody events they had witnessed.

Led by one such jack of spades, the two Parisians entered a large inner courtyard with a group of visitors. The warder pointed out the 'Bloody Tower', where Edward's children were murdered; Beauchamp Tower, used as a state prison, where Jane Grey and Anne Boleyn were incarcerated; and Wakefield Tower, where Henry VII[1] was assassinated.

Supposedly built by William the Conqueror, the Tower is the embodiment of the English spirit. (p. 199)

The fortress has had its share of murders, the main political weapon at the disposal of English sovereigns, who did not scruple to wield it against their relatives and noblemen until the history of England was written in blood.

The visitors entered the Armouries, where a ridiculous array of armour was displayed on dummies representing English kings. The dummies strike ludicrous postures; one threatens the ceiling with a lance, another raises his mace as if to dash out his steed's brains, while a third wields an axe which will chop off his left arm if he is not careful. All this is in lamentable taste, more in keeping with a sideshow in a fairground than the archaeological riches of a museum.

In the Queen Elizabeth arsenal, visitors can see the two axes, each on its block, which beheaded Anne Boleyn and the Earl of Essex. Jacques shuddered as he stroked the historic steel blades and counted on the blocks the marks left by royal politics.

The two young men left the Tower without lingering to count the cannon slumbering in the courtyard. As it was getting late, they walked back towards London Bridge after having had their passports stamped in King William Street, and ran to a landing-stage to catch a *waterman* as on the previous day. Instead of getting off at Westminster Bridge, they stayed on the steamboat and continued under the new Parliament Bridge. And there, as the boat emerged from under an arch spiked with scaffolding, they saw the splendid riverside façade of Westminster Hall stretched out along the Thames, just like in Justin Ouvrié's painting.[2] The pen falters, words stumble, unable to capture the overwhelming majesty of the spectacle. One might be a thousand leagues from London. Architectural lines of great purity emphasize the harmony and regularity of the proudly emblazoned façade. Victoria Tower and the

They saw the splendid riverside façade of Westminster Hall stretched out along the Thames. (p. 200)

Clock Tower rise at either end of the mighty, tranquil building. The river glides below. The sight is fair indeed and it is hard to tear oneself away.

The banks along this stretch of the Thames are picturesque and varied. Opposite the Houses of Parliament, Lambeth Palace is a pleasant medley of irregular gardens, tree-shaded lawns and buildings. The architecture juxtaposes different styles, periods and kinds of building, all however in the 'Anglo-Saxon' manner. Overall, Lambeth Palace is a corner of medieval England forgotten on the edge of the Thames. It is the London residence of the Archbishop of Canterbury; London has only a Bishop. When Scottish presbyterians and puritans pass by the luxurious palace, they turn their heads in scorn.

The steamboat stopped at Vauxhall Bridge, in Lambeth. As they disembarked at the Millbank landing-stage, Jacques showed Jonathan an extraordinary building situated on the left bank. It was the Penitentiary, a sinister-looking prison. London's jails are all equally frightful. This one is a gigantic, massive tomb where criminals who would formerly have been deported, are locked up for life.

An hour's drive by cab took the two Parisians to Regent's Park, for a quick glimpse. They were in search of fleeting impressions which memory and fantasy would eventually fix more durably in their minds. To reach the park, they crossed the most beautiful districts of London. In Pimlico, fine houses with big windows line the streets with a distinguished air of prosperity and ease. Most overlook shaded squares with a central garden for the exclusive use of local residents. Belgrave Square is built in a quiet uniform style with no shops. The large, handsome buildings look like peaceful mansions a hundred leagues from the docks and the City.

The cab left them at Park Square, outside Regent's Park, a huge expanse of 450 acres dotted with stately homes, criss-crossed with wide tree-lined drives and covered with extensive lawns. The grounds contain the Zoological Gardens and the Botanical Gardens but Jonathan refused to visit either. He collapsed on one of the park's high green benches which defy the usual English sense of comfort. It was time to bring their whirlwind tour to an end. Their forced marches across the city, the weariness of their eyes and a sense of mental surfeit brought on by so many new sights and experiences had resulted in utter exhaustion. With a great effort, propping and cheering each other up, the two young men managed to reach Regent Street. The elegant street was crowded with vehicles. It was the hour when London's opulent society went on parade. Shops overflowed with women whose fine clothes account for the city's 40 000 milliners.

Jacques could not bear the idea of dining in their little alehouse: exhaustion and hunger made it seem three times as distant as it was.

Fortunately, he discovered a French restaurant. (p. 202)

Fortunately, he discovered a French restaurant at the Quadrant. He led his friend indoors and they spent the next two hours fighting hunger and exhaustion with all the means at their disposal. The food was French, but there was a little English air about it.

Notes

1 In fact Henry VI.
2 The painting referred to here is *Le Parlement* (1850) by Justin Ouvrié, a painter and lithographer born in Paris in 1806. He travelled extensively in England, Germany, Holland and Italy, as well as France, taking sketches. A landscape painter, he was also known for his city scenes which were available as paintings and lithographs. In 1836 he painted *l'Abbaye de Westminster* and *le Château de Twickenham*. In 1850, in addition to *Le Parlement*, he painted *l'Eglise de Westminster* and *la Chapelle de Lambeth à Londres*.

46

Madame Tussaud's

'SO THIS IS THE END of our great journey,' Jonathan said over the dessert.

'We've certainly seen a lot,' Jacques said. 'I should think our eyes have had their fill.'

'I must admit I'll be glad to get back to Paris. I've reached such a degree of saturation I can't take in another thing. My senses are worn threadbare.'

'I can almost agree with you. Just one more effort and you can relax.'

'One more! There's still something to visit?'

'Don't be alarmed. I'm determined to do everything on my programme and this is the last item. Come on!'

'Where to, in heaven's name?'

'Wait and see.'

'I don't like the sound of that.'

'Come on!'

'Well, if you insist.'

Like two weary pilgrims, they resumed their wandering. It was eight in the evening and the streets were already dark. Jacques had carefully studied his plan of London and without hesitating he turned left off Regent Street, up broad Oxford Street, which he followed as far as Baker Street, ignoring his friend's questions.

He paused outside a Protestant chapel. This, he reassured Jonathan, was not their goal, but he insisted on glancing in. The dimly-lit chapel looked gloomy and austere. A few people sat scattered in the wooden pews, plunged in motionless silence. At the far end, standing at a lectern lit by a small lamp, a minister was reading aloud from the Bible. His grave, monotonous voice sent the words echoing mournfully round the depressing room. The puritanical chill froze the senses and penetrated to the bone.

'Let's get out of here,' Jacques said.

Jonathan shivered. 'We should never have gone in.'

A short distance away, higher up Baker Street, people were converging on a brightly-lit entrance. Jacques headed towards it, asking Jonathan for two shillings. They received two tickets in exchange and entered a dazzling room.

'Where are we?' Jonathan asked.

'At Madame Tussaud's, the granddaughter of the famous Curtius.'

'What! In a waxwork shop?'

'No, in a museum you've never seen the like of before. Look!'

The rooms were crowded and but for the bright period costumes, it would have been difficult to tell hosts and guests apart.

The exhibition brought together lifesize waxworks of figures past and present. The British court was represented in full pomp: sovereigns, princesses, duchesses, all the highly-placed persons of the realm were there, absorbed in quiet conversation. Bosoms gleamed with medals, ribbons, crosses and the whole hierarchy of official decorations. Diamonds twinkled in the tresses of queens and on the swordhilts of kings. The court of France was there too, in full apparel. Two huge rooms were scarcely big enough to contain such a gathering of high society. The whole display of kings appointed by Napoleon looked a little drab in this glittering array of crowned heads.

Present-day personalities stood in the centre of the rooms, while in window recesses and on platforms along the walls the ancestors of the English court posed and paraded. There was that huge Henry VIII strutting in the midst of his six wives, Catherine of Aragon, Anne Boleyn, Jane Seymour, Anne of Cleves, Catherine Howard and Catherine Parr; the huge butcher looked horrid surrounded by his unfortunate victims. Further on was Mary Queen of Scots in all the magic of her beauty. Such was the perfection of those waxwork masterpieces that the reality cannot have been more arresting. The loveliness of the Scottish queen surpassed anything that could be dreamed up by the most ardent imagination.

Jacques and Jonathan found it difficult to make their way through these flesh-and-wax crowds. They came upon a brand-new Garibaldi surrounded by human admirers and, a short distance away, found William Pitt and Sheridan placidly discussing like English aristocrats.

Jacques turned to a visitor who was staring at him to ask the name of a striking churchman seated in a splendid chair. Obtaining no reply and thinking the man had not understood, he asked Jonathan to repeat the question.

Jonathan was no more successful. Jacques was beginning to feel angry when a bystander started laughing. They had been talking to a waxwork!

Such is the perfection of those figures that visitors are easily led astray. Many waxworks are represented in modern dress and they stand not on platforms but on the floor, mingling with the crowd that eddies around them. But Jonathan was caught when he stared at the face and pinched the arm of a gentleman who was very much alive and not one of Madame Tussaud's heroes.

Adjoining the two main rooms is an exhibition of objects that formerly belonged to Napoleon. Most of them were collected at Waterloo. They include the vehicle in which the betrayed and beaten Emperor left the battlefield. Every visitor, man, woman and child, made a point of entering the vehicle and sitting there for a while before coming out again, proud and happy. It was an endless procession that Jacques and Jonathan abstained from joining.

47

Guillotine, English-style

'I T'S ALL VERY INTERESTING,' Jonathan said, 'but I wish there were chairs for us as well as for those waxwork chaps.'

'Be patient. Just get out twelve pence and follow me.'

'Again!'

'After that, you'll be free.'

At the far end of the second room they found a doorway through which the crowd was surging. It opened into a third room, large, dimly-lit, hung with dark curtains.

A quick glance set the Parisians shivering. Two or three hundred heads were carefully lined on shelves, staring at the visitors with sinister eyes. Each head had been carefully cast and labelled; each bore the hideous stamp of crime and suffering. Here were the dreadful features of La Bocarmi, Lacenaire, Castaing, Papavoine, Peytel, Mme Lafarge, Bastide, Jorion, Benoît, Palmer, Burke; America, France, England and other nations had contributed their share of lopped heads to this appalling collection. The sight of them revived the memories of the violent crimes their perpetrators had paid for with their lives, creating an uncanny atmosphere.

In the middle of the room, Marat had just been stabbed by Charlotte Corday and lay dying in his bath. Blood still flowed from his gaping wound. Nearby, Fieschi was setting his infernal machine on fire. Other criminals stood in the shadows, talking. Orsini and Pieri mingled with the crowd. One ended up wondering whether one might not oneself belong to this company of scoundrels. Hands quivered and eyes grew bloodshot at the very thought.

'Where are we?'

'In the Chamber of Horrors.'

'I'm not sure it's in very good taste.'

'Well, it's all very English. But look here!'

'The guillotine!'

Indeed, that dreadful instrument rose at the far end of the room, the first mechanical device to be applied to the execution of political policy! And it was not just any guillotine! It was the one of 1793, which had felt so many victims trembling in its steel embrace, which had chopped off the heads of Louis XVI and Robespierre, Marie-Antoinette and Madame Dubarry, Danton and André Chénier, Philippe Egalité and Saint-Just. An unquestionably genuine certificate bearing reliable signatures hung on the guillotine, attesting that Samson himself had sold it after the Revolution and the Reign of Terror. Nothing could be more authentic – or more bloodcurdling!

The scaffold was ready. The crowd pressed up the steps. Dragging his friend along, Jacques followed. They reached the platform from which two red posts rose, supporting a trapeziform knife-blade. An iron bar fastened to one of the posts at shoulder height supported the heavy steel blade; the whole was fastened by a padlock in case some visitor had the bright idea of operating the mechanism.

In front of the posts stood the dreadful plank, awaiting its next victim. Jacques could not resist standing on the step leading up to it. As, horrified, he admired the grim simplicity of the device, all of a sudden there were stifled cries and a sound of choking. Everyone froze and stared at the terrifying blade. It had not moved. But a fat Englishman, bolder and more inquisitive than the rest, had decided to push his head through the circular lunette of the guillotine. He was stuck there, unable to pull his head out, choking under the pressure of the top plank. Jacques dashed up and raised it: the semicircular opening was banded with iron and it had squeezed the poor man's neck. He groaned with satisfaction when Jacques rescued him.

'Well,' Jacques said, 'I've made a comforting discovery. With that machine you're more likely to be strangled before you're guillotined.'

'Thanks for telling me! That's most reassuring.'

'And now, after this last discovery, we can go. One last look and we'll leave England, saying goodbye to France's guillotine.'

Back in the street they breathed in the evening air with the relief of condemned men who have been granted a pardon on the scaffold.

A cab gathered them up and left them an hour later, more than half asleep, at the London Bridge Hotel. The next morning they went to the Brighton Railway Station on Duke Street. With the help of an interpreter they arranged their journey and saw to it that their portmanteaux were safely taken care of. Then they climbed into a first-class compartment.

As the train passed over the housetops, Jacques glanced for the last time at the Thames and at St Paul's Cathedral. He caught sight of the magical Crystal Palace of Sydenham,[1] although it was only a fleeting glimpse. Two hours later the train stopped in Brighton, that Naples of the North so warmly praised by Thackeray. A branch-line links Brighton to the small port of Newhaven, which they reached half an hour later, to find the two huge funnels of the *Orléans* already belching smoke in preparation for the crossing to France.

The two young men hurried on deck.

'Well, here's goodbye to England,' Jacques said.

'For ever! For ever!' Jonathan added.

Without delay, the steamer raised anchor and set its course for Dieppe. The sea was smooth and the crossing swift. After five hours the cliffs of France appeared on the horizon.

'Do you feel anything on seeing France again?' Jacques asked.

'No,' Jonathan said. 'Do you?'

'No. Nothing at all.'

Note

¹ Built for the Great Exhibition of 1851, destroyed by fire in 1936. Curiously, Verne does not refer to it by name here, but as 'palais féerique' (fairy palace).

48

They will travel in their memories

S O IT IS OVER at last, that epic journey to England and Scotland. Despite all the obstacles, problems, delays, worries; despite some anxiety, even despair and misunderstanding: it is over.

After seventeen days stranded in Bordeaux and a four-day sea voyage to Liverpool, Jacques and Jonathan spent barely a week wandering in curious regions of the United Kingdom. What will survive of this swift journey, this frantic rush, this bird's-eye view? Will the young men have brought home enough at least to fill sweet hours of leisure and relaxation?

They will have ventured into the Atlantic, sailed along the French and British coasts, travelled up and down England and crossed the Tweed, to stride through Scotland. They will have felt Liverpool and formed an impression of Edinburgh; they will have glimpsed Glasgow, guessed at Stirling, groped at London. They will have touched mountains and skimmed over lakes, imagined if not recognized new customs, geographical variations, strange manners, national differences. They will have sensed much – but, in truth, seen nothing!

Only now, on their return, can their serious exploration begin, for imagination will henceforth be their guide as they travel backwards through their memories.

Afterword
from the Editor of the French edition

A frequent subject of conversation in the Verne household was Allott, the Scottish ancestor from whom Jules Verne's maternal great-uncle, Prudent Allotte de la Fuÿe, claimed to be descended. According to him, this Allott had come over from Scotland to serve as an archer in the guard of King Louis XI. The great-uncle may well have been influenced by Scott's *Quentin Durward*, since a similar story forms the basis of the plot. Nonetheless, he found an enthusiastic audience in his niece, Sophie Verne, and in his great-nephews who soaked in his passion for Scotland and its history, customs and literature.

In this, the great-uncle was a man of his times. From 1827 onwards, English travellers headed north for Scotland, soon followed by tourists from the continent. Their excursions took them to Fingal's Cave, the Hebrides, the Highlands and Edinburgh, reflecting the contemporary fascination for a region glowingly praised by the poets and artists of the Romantic Movement. Walter Scott's success had contributed decisively to this enthusiasm and guidebooks traced all the places he described in his novels. Scotland also inspired continental composers and artists: Beethoven's Scottish melodies; Mendelssohn's Scottish Symphony and Hebrides (or Fingal's Cave) Overture; Chateaubriand's protagonist René, amongst other great wanderings, made a visit to the land of the Bard Ossian; Charles Nodier's *Voyage* and the writings of Amédée Pichot; basic reference books for Frenchmen setting out for the country of the MacGregors: all these works conjured up idealized picturesque impressions of Scotland for Europe's cultural élite.

A Romantic Journey

Jules Verne already shared the Scottish fascination of his time when in 1859 he undertook a journey to the land of his ancestor. As he told Marie A Belloc, 40 years later, in an interview for the *Strand Magazine:*

'All my life I have delighted in the works of Sir Walter Scott, and during a never-to-be forgotten tour in the British Isles, my happiest days were spent in Scotland. I still see, as in a vision, beautiful, picturesque Edinburgh, with its Heart of Midlothian and many entrancing memories; the Highlands, world-forgotten Iona, and the wild Hebrides. Of course, to one familiar with the works of Scott, there is scarce a district of his native land lacking some association connected with the writer and his immortal work.'[1]

Like his main character in *Voyage à reculons*, the endearing Jacques Lavaret, Verne had read virtually the whole of Scott long before starting on his journey. References to novels which inspired Balzac are scattered through *Voyage à reculons en Angleterre et en Ecosse* ('Backwards to Britain'), and are worked into Verne's later, 'Scottish' novels: *Le Rayon vert* ('The Green Ray') and *Les Indes noires* ('The Child of the Cavern'). The strange atmosphere of the latter, which takes place in the mines of Aberfoyle, suggests that Verne had also read *Trilby*, a fantastic tale by Nodier set on the shores of Loch Katrine. When he came to write *Voyage à reculons* ('Backwards to Britain'), Verne curiously chose to devote his opening paragraph to Nodier's comparison between Scotland and the Jura in the *Cycle du dériseur sensé*. Even before embarking on the *Extraordinary Journeys*, Verne was drawn to Scotland by a desire to explore in real life the places he had discovered in fiction, and thus to renew and prolong the delights Scott's novels had produced in him. This feedback between travel and literature heightens Jacques's and Jonathan's interest in a performance of *Macbeth*, which they see in London on their way back. Literary memories – they had read the play in France – overlap here with geographical memories. And what can be more exhilarating than to have visited a place where Shakespeare set one of his tragedies? A first-hand knowledge of the setting combines with a new reading, or performance of, an admired masterpiece in a blend of enriching impressions.

However attractive, a literary pilgrimage was not the sole purpose of Verne's journey. Like many fellow travellers of the Romantic Period, he found in his travels countless opportunities to satisfy his curiosity. His interest in Scotland's historic buildings was sharpened by the country's numerous links with France, first under Mary, Queen of Scots, then in the early 19th century, when Charles X sought refuge in Holyrood and captive officers of Napoleon's army served as tutors in Scottish households.[2] Music was another source of interest. Besides fostering pleasant contacts between the guests and their warm, hospitable hosts, it has surprises in store for Jonathan, the composer accompanying Jacques. He is attracted by the melancholy beauty of Scottish music and delighted by a piper's fine variations. So-called popular music appealed to the Romantics, owing to their conviction that all men, and more especially artists, are equal. Untutored exponents of a given art were admired for their native unspoilt talents, which curious amateurs set out to discover, anticipating, as it were, present-day ethnologists. Convinced that a chain of cause and effect produces particular characteristics, the Romantics sought picturesque confirmation in geography, history and travellers' accounts of customs, costumes and beliefs.

Hence the texts and guidebooks which Verne freely admits to having consulted, through the intermediary of his alter ego, Jacques Lavaret, before embarking with Aristide Hignard,[3] alias Jonathan Savournon, during the summer of 1859. The author and his friend benefited from a discount, thanks to Aristide's brother, who worked in a travel agency. Travel authors mentioned in *Voyage à reculons* ('Backwards to Britain') include Jean-Baptiste Richard, author of guidebooks providing detailed descriptions of European tours, and Louis Enault, an interesting personality of the time who had travelled throughout Europe between 1848 and 1851; he had just published his *Angleterre, Ecosse, Irlande, voyage pittoresque* ('England, Scotland, Ireland: a Picturesque Journey'), which Verne mentions here. For his descriptions of London, Verne borrowed, heavily, at times, from Francis Wey's *Les Anglais chez eux/Esquisses de voyage*, which appeared in the magazine *Musée des familles* from November 1850 to May 1851. During the same period, Verne was a contributor to the magazine, whose founder was Pitre-Chevalier,[4] a fellow citizen from Nantes, and he may have had it in mind, eight years later, for a possible serialization of *Voyage à reculons* ('Backwards to Britain').

Literature, history – social observation, too, had its appeal and Verne did not hesitate to make his characters encounter the material and moral misery rampant in major industrial cities. His grim picture of Liverpool bears comparisons with Alexis de Tocqueville's famous impressions of Manchester,[5] while his descriptions of urban poverty and attempts to find explanations for it recall travel-accounts by other writers of the time, notably economists, politicians and journalists who travelled too, like the poets and artists, keeping careful accounts of their journeys. Jacques and Jonathan travel under the guidance of Verne the journalist, who does not shrink from discussing issues such as urban insalubrity and prostitution. This boldness totally vanished when he turned to fiction, where beggars are reduced to a miserable female figure fleetingly encountered by Phileas Fogg as he enters Charing Cross Station.

In many respects a journalistic account, this manuscript, unpublished until 1989, offers unexpected personal insights and a truthful transcription of Verne's first journey to the British Isles. Having set out with no precise literary project – the same occurred again later with his cruises in the Atlantic and the Mediterranean which inspired *Une Ville flottante* ('A Floating City') and *Mathias Sandorf* – the writer has left us a travel diary that has the refreshing vigour of a sketchbook.

Verne's Sketchbook of Britain

Happy memories of this first journey to Britain led Verne north again several times in the course of his life. In the spring of 1867 he returned to Liverpool, this time with his brother, to embark for the United States aboard the *Great Eastern*, the renamed *Leviathan* which had amazed him when he had first seen it on the Thames eight years earlier. The following year he wrote *Vingt mille lieues sous les mers* ('Twenty Thousand Leagues Under the Sea') and, like Aronnax, sailed to London in his modest yacht, the *Saint-Michel I*. Ten years later, in July 1879, the proud owner of a magnificent yacht, the *Saint-Michel III*, whose home port was Nantes, Verne set sail from his native town for his second, and almost certainly his last, voyage to Scotland, in the company of his son Michel and one of the latter's friends. Verne and his wife had had serious problems with Michel, hence the idea perhaps of retracing with the son a route that had formerly delighted the father – this journey helps to refute the view long held by his biographers that he lacked all practical pedagogic instinct. Once in Scotland, did Verne visit the famous Fingal's cave, which is the setting for *Le Rayon vert* ('The Green Ray'), published in 1882? Questioned on this point towards the end of his life, Verne sometimes seemed a little vague. Even if he never landed on the island of Staffa, the many descriptions and illustrations available in the reviews at the time would have been enough to stimulate him, since he also travelled extensively in his imagination.

Verne used *Voyage à reculons* ('Backwards to Britain') as a quarry, reworking his bold, picturesque observations on cities and landscapes to create the settings for several of his novels. It was from Liverpool that Captain Hatteras set sail for the North Pole, and that the leading characters in *Une Ville flottante* ('A Floating City') embarked for their crossing to the United States. *Les Enfants du Capitaine Grant* (Captain Grant's Children) and *Les Forceurs du blocus* ('The Blockade Runners') started from Glasgow. London was the port of embarkation for Dr Fergusson, then for Phileas Fogg, who bought the *Henrietta* from Captain Speedy, the namesake of the captain of the *Hamburg* in *Backwards to Britain*. In Liverpool, Jacques and Jonathan meet Mr Joe Kennedy; in *Cinq semaines en ballon* ('Five Weeks in a Balloon'), we have Joe and Dick Kennedy who accompany the bold aeronaut. Thus Verne used the manuscript *Backwards to Britain* as a sketchbook,

216

lifting names, descriptions and characters which he then altered for his novels.

Scottish elements recur throughout his work. In *The Green Ray*, one finds sporadic references to the Highland costume recalling those in chapter 35 of this book. Jacques's and Jonathan's rainy journey up the Firth of Forth on board the *Prince of Wales* is later made by the engineer Starr, on the same steamship, when he returns to the mines of Aberfoyle at the beginning of *Les Indes noires* ('The Child of the Cavern');[6] while the excursion to Edinburgh and Loch Katrine and its environs proposed to Nell in the same novel was originally the one described in *Backwards to Britain*.

Jonathan's talents as a musician are displayed in Mr B—'s drawing-room where he gladly entertains his hosts at the piano. When Miss Amelia teaches him Scottish tunes he discovers that he can play them using 'the black keys only' (Chapter 24). In *Twenty Thousand Leagues Under the Sea*, Captain Nemo plays the organ in the same way: 'The captain's fingers ran over the keyboard and I noticed that he used the black keys only, thus giving his tunes an essentially Scottish sound.' This poetic interlude comes straight out of Verne's 'sketchbook' of Scottish memories.

Other sketches are apparent in his work. Here and there, details reveal how his first journey to Britain remained lodged in his imagination. Thus Jacques keeps a log-book, preceding in this Aronnax who is presented as the real author of *Twenty Thousand Leagues Under the Sea*. Just as later Nemo's prisoner visited the *Nautilus*, Jacques and Jonathan visit Oakley Castle, where they note the natural history display, the rich library, and the powerful scientific instruments. Anxiety over a sandbank in the Loire (in Chapter 4) makes Jacques think of the reefs of Vanikoro in French Polynesia, which later worry the occupants of the *Nautilus*. In his very first account of a journey, Verne reveals what proved to be a lasting fascination for the sea and its natural phenomena, such as phosphorescence (in Chapter 9).

Fact or fiction?

Poised between fact and fiction, *Voyage à reculons* ('Backwards to Britain') belongs to that unclassifiable genre which includes works like George Sand's *Un hiver à Majorque* ('Winter in Majorca', trans Robert Graves, London, 1956), a book that cannot decide whether it is a novel or a travel-account. During the Romantic Movement, travel-writing ranged freely from the factual accounts which we have become used to, to unrestrained fantasies with fanciful titles such as *Voyage en zigzag*[7] ('Zigzag Journey') or *Voyage où il vous plaira*[8] ('Journey Where You Please'). Others still were a mixture of styles, with the author, in the guise of a wanderer-philosopher, indulging in reflections and meditations on a whole range of subjects inspired by his travels as in *Letters of a Traveller*. In many respects, this last category of travel-writing reached back to the essays and discourses of the Age of Enlightenment. In all three kinds of travel-writing, authors did not worry about over-rigid frameworks, preferring to keep an impression of spontaneity and personal account and to alter their tone and style as they pleased.

In Verne's writings, the poetry of travel is to be found in the thrills of novelty and in a fascination with exhilarating speed and varied means of locomotion. Jacques's reactions as he travels north to Scotland are imbued with a poetry recalling that of Victor Hugo.[9] Visual emotion – scenery 'which provides the eye with a new sensation of colour' (Chapter 18) – is followed by the magic of fantastic speed: 'The train rushed along a precipitous track that clung to the cliff-face of those old rocks. The dizzy speed was almost supernatural and at each bend the train seemed about to throw itself into the ravine where the black waters of a torrent raged' (Chapter 18).

The train journey to London acquires fantastic tints: 'Jonathan could not sleep and at Newcastle, through a half-open window, he glimpsed a terrifying nightscape. The kingdom of coal was ablaze. Plumes of fire flickered above the tall factory chimneys; these are the trees of this dirty black region, and they form an immense forest, illuminated by wild, tawny reflections' (Chapter 37). Powerful sensations of this kind make up for occasional physical discomfort which the two young men endure good-humouredly, even though they prefer the comfort of a ship's cabin or saloon whenever this is available (Chapter 11). As to means of locomotion, Jacques and Jonathan use all those available in the mid-19th century. Journeys by train, river-, and ocean-going steamer, omnibus and coach alternate with long walks, each imposing its own rhythm on the different stages of this varied, picturesque journey which prefigures the euphoria, if not the urgency, of Phileas Fogg's dash around the world.

The setbacks and delays which constantly oblige the young men to postpone their departure and, once they set off, the tight schedule which ensues, reducing leisureliness to a minimum, make their travels appear rather like an anti-journey. Hence the initial idea of calling the book *Voyage à reculons* ('Backwards to Britain'), in a vein akin to Sterne's *Tristram Shandy*, a book Verne was fond of (he mentions it in the opening chapter), and where the hero is not born until quite a way into the book.[10] He had the same idea for a title for *César Cascabel*, where a circus troop anxious to leave the United States for France is constantly driven westwards by chance instead.[11] Other characters such as Paganel, Uncle Prudent and Kéraban find themselves being forced into 'involuntary journeys' by setbacks which alter their initial projects.[12] As a result, what starts out as a straightforward journey twists and turns, shaping the plot in the most unexpected fashion. In *Voyage à reculons* ('Backwards to Britain') this creates an approximately &-shaped trajectory.[13] To create these amusing variations, Verne preferred the charm of leisurely comings and goings to the panache and briskness of straight-line routes. 'You never travel so far as when you don't know where you're going,' Jacques notes wisely and ironically, long before the same conclusion is reached by characters in *Le Rayon vert* ('The Green Ray'), *Bourses de Voyages* ('Travelling Scholarships'), *L'Agence Thompson and Co* ('The Thompson Travel Agency'), *Clovis Dardentor* and *Claudius Bombarnac.*

Other traits of the two characters' personality reappear in later works. Hector Servadac, too, will chuckle over a map of Britain which looks like a caricature of an old woman.[14] Like Jacques and Jonathan, others will enjoy good meals spiced with lively conversation and indulge in puns and word-games inspired by foreign languages. They are interested in natural phenomena such as the aurora borealis and echoes. They are attracted by the advances of modern civilization, and particularly fascinated by the ports of Nantes, Bordeaux, London and Glasgow, where steamers of all kinds throng. There is nothing affected in their fascination, which reveals a spontaneous delight in novelty, and Jacques takes an eager interest in technical devices such as pistons and oscillating engines. Verne's descriptions of the technological world are not devoid of humour, as when he describes 'the mechanical menagerie' of Liverpool docks, with its 'crabs [and] cranes' (Chapter 15).

Who operates this well-regulated world, if not those 'lifeless machines' Jacques and Jonathan meet in the course of a meal which ends in blows (Chapter 16) and those 'jacks of spades' who have been guarding the Tower like clockwork figures since the 15th century? (Chapter 45). Unsurprisingly, machines have imposed their rhythms on men in a land from where Phileas Fogg sets out with such determination. Mechanical devices have a fearful magnetism, to the extent of causing an English visitor to slip his head through the lunette of the guillotine on show at Madame Tussaud's (Chapter 47). The imagination of the British expands with their unrivalled technical inventiveness. Who else, Verne notes with wry amusement, could have thought of designing unrealisable machines to carry out the siege of Sebastopol? Just as eccentric is the 'unusual steam-operated machine' Jacques and Jonathan discover in Glasgow: 'it was very ingenious: a live pig was placed at one

end and it came out at the other in the form of appetizing sausages'
(Chapter 31).

Similarly, automation seems to regulate the production of mental
nourishment. Music plays an important role here (as it does throughout
Verne's work), often in a context of mockery. The absurdly recurring
tunes from *Il Trovatore* create an irreverent musical catch phrase played
by instruments ranging from 'a cornet covered in a thick layer of
verdigris' (Chapter 17) to the 'gigantic organ with 80 stops and a steam-
powered swell' the two young men discover in St George's Hall, in
Liverpool (Chapter 17). But is the tone not set at the beginning when
Jacques hears on Austerlitz Bridge a barrel-organ mechanically
delivering the notes of Verdi's opera? The various mechanical
inventions that chart the two tourists' journey provide not only means of
conveyance but entertainment and amusement.

Thus fantasy and humour colour a keen sense of observation already
apparent in *Voyage à reculons* ('Backwards to Britain'), prefiguring the
various directions Verne's writing took following his encounter with the
publisher P J Hetzel. Verne knows how to share with his readers
moments of boundless enthusiasm for the natural wonders of the world
and to convey the delights and astonishments of travel and exploration.
It is this stimulating blend that has confirmed Verne's pre-eminence in a
literary genre he made his own: the Journey.

Christian Robin
University of Nantes, 1989

Notes

[1] Verne, *Textes oubliés*, Union générale d'édition, 1979, p 361.

[2] A valuable account of this latter period is to be found in Margaret I
Bain's *Les Voyageurs français en Ecosse (1770–1830)* (French travellers
in Scotland, 1770–1830), Paris, Champion, 1931, pp 69–101.

[3] A composer and the son of a shipowner, Aristide Hignard shared
Verne's beginnings as a playwright. He composed the music for
several of Verne's poems, which were published in successive
editions under the title *Rimes et mélodies* (Rhymes and Melodies). The
second collection included 'Souvenirs d'Ecosse' – the words of this
song appear in chapter 18 of *Les Indes noires* ('The Child of the
Cavern') (1877).

[4] Pitre-Chevalier (also known as Pierre Chevalier), 1812–63. A
journalist, editor of the *Figaro*, then owner of the *Musée des familles*,
Pitre-Chevalier never broke off ties with his home-town Nantes. His
wife had a salon in Marly-le-Roy, where Verne was a regular visitor
during his Parisian years. It was thanks to his contacts with Pitre-
Chevalier that Verne published his early works: in 1851, *Les Châteaux
en Californie*, a play the two men wrote together, and two short stories,
'Un drame au Mexique' ('A Drama in Mexico'), 'Un voyage en
ballon' ('Journey in a Balloon'); in 1852, 'Martin Paz'; in 1854,

'Maître Zacharius' ('Master Zacharius'). (See Luce Courville, 'Pitre-Chevalier', *Cahiers du Centre d'Etudes verniennes et du Musée Jules Verne*, n° 6, Nantes, 1986, pp 34–47).

5 *Voyage en Angleterre et en Irlande* (Journey to England and Ireland) (1833–5), Paris, édition Idées Gallimard, 1982, pp 184–92.

6 The engineer's journey is slightly longer than the one Jacques and Jonathan make.

7 By the Swiss-German author, Rodolphe Töpffer (1844). The book is at once instructive and entertaining.

8 By Tony Johannot, Alfred de Musset and P J Hetzel, Verne's publisher (1843). A study of this book by P C Taittinger is to be found in *Métamorphoses du récit de voyage* ('Transformations in Travel Fiction'), edited by F Moureau (preface by Pierre Brunel), Champion-Slatkine, Paris-Geneva, 1986, pp 110–15. *Voyage où il vous plaira* ('Journey Where You Please') includes a scene where a magical clock breaks and this may have inspired Verne in *Maître Zacharius* ('Master Zacharius'). The travellers are two young men, Frantz and Walter, like Jacques and Jonathan, and their journey naturally includes Scotland and England.

9 Especially *Voyage en Belgique* ('Journey to Belgium') (written in 1837), which Verne cannot have read, since Hugo's letters were not published until 1892.

10 'Sterne, of whom I am a great reader and admirer also': Verne to Robert H Sherard, 'Jules Verne Revisited', *T P's Weekly*, 9 Oct 1903.

11 See the first page of the manuscript of *César Cascabel*, in the Bibliothèque Municipale de Nantes.

12 'Involuntary journeys' were in Verne's day a variation on adventure stories. The first of a series bearing that title, *Voyage involontaire*, was published by Lucien Biart in *Magasin d'éducation et de récréation*, in 1878–9.

13 Also &-shaped is the entrance to the grotto occupied by the air-wrecked party in *L'Ile mystérieuse* ('The Mysterious Island') (Part 1, chapter 4). On this interaction of typography and topography, see C Robin, *Un Monde connu et inconnu: Jules Verne* (Jules Verne: a Known and Unknown World), Nantes, Vanden Brugge, 1978, p 232.

14 Chapter 21, p 118. See also *Hector Servadac*, Part 2, chapter 19. 'It was indeed Europe spread out below. They could recognize states by the bizarre shapes nature and history had given them. Britain, a lady walking eastwards, in a dress with rumpled pleats and her head adorned with islands of all sizes.'

Bibliography

Butcher, William, 'Journey to the Centre of Inspiration', review in the *Times Higher Educational Supplement*, August 1990

Butcher, William, 'Jules Verne and Edinburgh', *Graffiti* [Edinburgh], no 3, Spring 1981, pp 7–10

Dumas, Olivier, *Jules Verne*, Lyon, La Manufacture, 1988, chapters entitled 'Paralysie faciale et boulimie', 'Mariage et boursicotage' and 'L'Écrivain maritime'

Dumas, Olivier, '*Voyage en Angleterre et en Ecosse*', la première grande œuvre de Jules Verne et le premier *Voyage à reculons*', *Bulletin de la Société Jules Verne* [*BSJV*], no 89, 1st Quarter 1989, pp 13–17

Dumas, Olivier, 'Un Faux *Voyage à reculons* dans une fausse malle', *BSJV*, no 93, 1st Quarter 1990, pp 6–7

Gazier, Michèle, review in *Télérama*, no 1050, 29 April to 5 May 1989

Jules-Verne, Jean, *Jules Verne*, Paris, Hachette, 1973, translated as *Jules Verne: a biography*, New York, Taplinger, and London, MacDonald and Jane's, 1976. Trans and adapted by Roger Greaves

P L, 'La Malle de Jules Verne', review in *Le Monde*, 28 April 1988

Woollen, Geoff, 'Jules Verne and Scotland', *Bulletin of the Franco-Scottish Society*, no 15, Sept 1991, pp 10–12

WB

A Chronology of Jules Verne's life[1]

1828   8 February: birth of Jules Verne, on the Ile Feydeau in Nantes, to Pierre Verne, a lawyer and son and grandson of lawyers, and Sophie, née Allotte de la Fuÿe, from a military line.

1829   Birth of brother, Paul, who became a naval officer, but retired in 1859 to take up the profession of stockbroker; followed by those of sisters Anna (1836), Mathilde (1839) and Marie (1842).

1834–8   Goes to school: the teacher, Mme Sambain, is the widow of a sea-captain, whose return she is still waiting for.

1838–41   Collège Saint-Stanislas. Performs well in geography, translation from Greek and Latin, and singing.

1841–6   Goes to Petit Séminaire, then to Lycée Royal de Nantes. Above average; probably won a prize in geography. Passes *baccalauréat* without difficulty. Writes poems and short pieces in prose.

1847   Studies law in Paris: at this time his cousin, Caroline Tronson, with whom he has been unhappily in love for several years, becomes engaged. Writes a play called *Alexandre VI*.

1848–9   June: revolution in Paris. Verne is present at the July disturbances. He continues his law studies, sharing a room at 24 Rue de l'Ancienne-Comédie. His uncle Châteaubourg introduces him into literary *salons*. Meets writers Alexandre Dumas *père* and *fils*. Writes a large number of plays, including *La Conspiration des poudres* (The Gunpowder Plot). Passes law degree. Father allows him to stay on in Paris.

1850   12 June: his one-act comedy *Les Pailles rompues* (Broken Straws) runs for 12 nights at Dumas's Théâtre Historique, and is published.

1851   Publishes short stories 'Un drame au Mexique' ('A Drama in Mexico') and 'Un drame dans les airs' ('Drama in the Air').

1852–5   Becomes secretary at Théâtre Lyrique. Publishes the short stories 'Martin Paz', 'Maître Zacharius' ('Master Zacharius'), 'Un hivernage dans les glaces' ('Winter in the Ice'); and the play *Les Châteaux en Californie* ('Castles in California') in collaboration with Pitre-Chevalier. His operette *Le Colin-maillard* ('Blind Man's Buff'), written with Michel Carré, is performed to music by Hignard.

1856   20 May: goes to a wedding in Amiens, and meets a young widow with two children, Honorine de Viane.

1857   10 January: marries Honorine, becomes a stockbroker in Paris, and moves house several times.

1859–60   Visits Scotland with Hignard. Writes *Voyage à reculons en Angleterre et en Ecosse* ('Backwards to Britain').

1861   Goes to Norway and Denmark with Hignard.

          3 August: birth of only child, Michel.

1863   31 January: *Cinq semaines en ballon* ('Five Weeks in a Balloon') appears, three months after first submission to publisher Jules Hetzel, and is an immediate success.

1864   Publication of 'Edgar Poe et ses œuvres' (Edgar Poe and his Works), *Voyages et aventures du Capitaine Hatteras* ('The Adventures of Captain Hatteras') and *Voyage au centre de la Terre* ('Journey to the Centre of the Earth'). (All dates are those of beginning of first publication in French, usually in serial form.) Gives up his unsuccessful stockbroker practice, and moves to Auteuil.

1865   *De la Terre à la Lune* ('From the Earth to the Moon'), and *Les Enfants du Capitaine Grant* (Captain Grant's Children). Death of Mme Estelle Duchêne of Asnières, close friend of Verne's.

1867   16 March: goes with brother Paul to Liverpool, thence on *Great Eastern* to United States.

1868   Buys a boat, *Saint-Michel*. Visits Southampton, Brighton and London.

1869   Rents a house in Amiens. Publishes *Vingt mille lieues sous les mers* ('Twenty Thousand Leagues Under the Sea'), and *Autour de la Lune* ('Round the Moon').

1870   Outbreak of Franco-Prussian War: Verne is coastguard at Le Crotoy (Somme).

1871   3 November: father dies.

1872   Moves to 44 Boulevard Longueville, Amiens; becomes member of Académie d'Amiens. Publication of *Le Tour du monde en quatre-vingts jours* ('Around the World in Eighty Days').

1874   *Une fantaisie du Docteur Ox* ('Dr Ox's Experiment, and Other Stories'), *L'Île mystérieuse* ('The Mysterious Island'), and *Le Chancellor* ('The Chancellor'). Begins collaboration with Adolphe d'Ennery on stage adaptation of novels (*Le Tour du monde en 80 jours* ('Around the World in Eighty Days'), performed 1874, *Les Enfants du Capitaine Grant* (Captain Grant's Children), 1878, *Michel Strogoff*, 1880; all highly successful).

1876–7   Publication of *Michel Strogoff* ('Michel Strogoff, the Courier of the Czar'), *Hector Servadac* and *Les Indes noires* ('The Child of the Cavern'). Buys second, then third boat, *Saint-Michel II* and *III* (a steam-yacht). Gives huge fancy-dress ball. Wife very seriously ill, but recovers.

1878   June–August: sails to Lisbon and Algiers.

1879–80   Publication of *Les Cinq cents millions de la Bégum* ('The Begum's Fortune'), *Les Tribulations d'un Chinois en Chine* ('The Tribulations of a Chinese Gentleman'), and *La Maison à vapeur* ('The Steam House'). Michel, who had caused problems throughout his childhood, marries an actress, despite the opposition of his father. Verne sails to Norway, Ireland and Scotland, including Edinburgh, Iona and Fingal's Cave.

1881   Publication of *La Jangada* ('The Giant Raft'). Sails to Rotterdam and Copenhagen.

1882   October: moves to a larger house at 2 Rue Charles-Dubois, Amiens. *Le Rayon vert* ('The Green Ray').

1883–4   Michel abducts a minor, Jeanne. Has two children by her within 11 months. Divorces his wife, and marries Jeanne. *Kéraban-le-Têtu* ('Kéraban the Inflexible'). Verne leaves with his wife for grand tour of Mediterranean, but cuts it short. On the way back, is probably received in private audience by Pope Leon XIII.

1885   8 March: another large fancy-dress ball. Publication of *Mathias Sandorf*.

1886   Publication of *Robur-le-Conquérant* ('The Clipper of the Clouds'). 15 February: sells *Saint-Michel III*.

9 March: his nephew Gaston, mentally ill, asks for money to travel to England. Verne refuses, and the nephew fires a pistol at him twice, making him lame for life.
17 March: Hetzel dies.

1887   15 February: mother dies.

1888   Is elected local councillor on a Republican list. For next 15 years attends council meetings, administrates theatre and fairs, opens Municipal Circus (1889), and gives public talks.

1889   *Sans dessus dessous* ('Topsy-Turvy') and 'In the Year 2889' (published in English in New York: signed Jules Verne but written by Michel, and then either translated or revised).

1890   Stomach problems.

1892   Publication of *Le Château des Carpathes* ('Carpathian Castle'). Pays debts for Michel.

1895   *L'Île à hélice* ('Propeller Island'), apparently the first novel written in a European language in the present tense and the third person.

1896–7 *Face au drapeau* ('For the Flag') and *Le Sphinx des glaces* ('An Antarctic Mystery'). Sued by chemist Turpin, inventor of melinite, who recognizes himself in the former novel. Successfully defended by Raymond Poincaré, future President of France. Health deteriorates (diabetes).
27 August: brother dies.

1899   Dreyfus Affair: Verne is anti-Dreyfusard, but approves of case being reviewed.

1900   Moves back into 44 Boulevard Longueville. Sight weakens (cataract).

1901   *Le Village aérien* ('The Village in the Treetops').

1904   *Maître du monde* ('The Master of the World').

1905   17 March: falls seriously ill.
24 March: dies, and is buried in Amiens.

1905–14 On his death, *L'Invasion de la mer* (Invasion of the sea) and *Le Phare du bout du monde* ('The Lighthouse at the End of the World') are in the process of publication. Michel takes responsibility for the remaining manuscripts, and publishes *Le Volcan d'or* ('The Golden Volcano') (1906), *L'Agence Thompson and Co* ('The Thompson Travel Agency') (1907), *La*

Chasse au météore ('The Hunt for the Meteor') (1908), *Le Pilote du Danube* ('The Danube Pilot') (1908), *Les Naufragés du Jonathan* ('Survivors of the Jonathan') (1909), *Le Secret de Wilhelm Storitz* ('The Secret of Wilhelm Storitz') (1910), *Hier et demain* ('Yesterday and Tomorrow') (short stories, including 'L'Eternel Adam' ('The Eternal Adam')) (1910) and *L'Etonnante aventure de la mission Barsac* ('The Barsac Mission') (1914). In 1978, it is proved that Michel in fact wrote considerable sections of these works, and in 1985-9 the original (ie Jules's) versions of most of them are published.

WB

Note

[1] Grateful acknowledgements are recorded to Oxford University Press for their kind permission to use this Chronology, first published in Jules Verne, *Voyage au centre de la Terre* ('Journey to the Centre of the Earth'). Translated with an Introduction and Notes by William Butcher ('World's Classics', 1992).